Traditional Aga Christmas

Traditional Aga Christmas

Louise Walker

A.

First published in Great Britain in 2005
by Absolute Press, an imprint of
Bloomsbury Publishing Plc

Absolute Press
Scarborough House
29 James Street West
Bath BA1 2BT
Phone 44 (0) 1225 316013
Fax 44 (0) 1225 445836
E-mail office@absolutepress.co.uk
Website www.absolutepress.co.uk

This new revised edition first published in 2013.

Text © Louise Walker
Photography © Mike Cooper
Snowflake illustrations
© Anja Kaiser - Fotolia.com

Publisher Jon Croft
Commissioning Editor Meg Avent
Art Director Matt Inwood
Project Editor Alice Gibbs
Photography Mike Cooper
Food Stylist Genevieve Taylor
Indexer Zoe Ross

A catalogue record of this book is available from
the British Library

A note about the text
This book was set using Century. The first
Century typeface was cut in 1894. In 1975 an
updated family of Century typefaces was
designed by Tony Stan for ITC.

ISBN 9781472903884

Printed in China by C&C Offset

Bloomsbury Publishing Plc
50 Bedford Square, London WC1B 3DP
www.bloomsbury.com

Contents

8 Introduction

10 Cooking in Advance

30 Christmas Eve

44 Christmas Day

70 Boxing Day

86 Lunches, Dinners and Suppers
    for the Festive Season

116 Cakes and Puddings

134 Entertaining

160 Christmas Leftovers

176 Kitchenalia

178 Appendices

184 Index

190 Acknowledgements

"The Aga, with its ability to add warmth and a welcoming feel to any kitchen, really comes into its own at Christmas."

Introduction

The Aga, with its ability to add warmth and a welcoming feel to any kitchen, really comes into its own at Christmas. It somehow epitomises the romantic image of the season of family gatherings and the giving and receiving of presents. Perhaps it is this that makes Christmas loom large in the minds of many Aga owners, especially new Aga owners facing their first Christmas, keen to entertain family and friends.

It is with this in mind that I have sectioned recipes in such a way that they will see you through the whole festive season. Of course, the secret to a relaxed Christmas is to do as much cooking and preparation as possible ahead of time, and therefore I have included in the Cooking in Advance chapter (page 10) all the classics such as Christmas Pudding, Christmas Cake and Mincemeat. For those of you who, even with the best will in the world, can not find time to prepare cakes in advance, turn to the Cakes and Puddings chapter (page 116) where you will find some delicious last minute recipes.

The Christmas Eve chapter (page 30) also includes all those dishes that, if cooked the day before, can make the day itself a lot less work and a lot more enjoyable. For Christmas Day, the classic turkey roast is of course here (see page 44), but for those who would like an alternative there are some wonderful pheasant, venison and goose dishes (see the Christmas Day chapter and also the Boxing Day chapter on page 70).

As everyone knows, entertaining at Christmas can be both great fun and extremely stressful! So if you are planning to have a party over the holiday period then you should turn to the Entertaining chapter on page 134 for a collection of easy and impressive nibbles and bites that should help you enjoy the festivities as much as your guests.

Cooking in Advance

If you can find the time to cook and store some of the dishes in this chapter before Christmas week it will not only save you valuable time and energy in the last few days leading up to Christmas, but will also give you a strong feeling of being in control. Of course, some dishes actually taste better if they are cooked in advance and left to mature.

Storing will allow flavours to develop, particularly Christmas cakes, puddings and mincemeat. October seems a good time to make them; comforting baking smells permeate the house and remind us all that Christmas is approaching. I know some people who go so far as to make two puddings in one year, eating one pudding and storing the other, and then the following year baking two cakes, eating one and then storing the other.

Always wrap your cakes in greaseproof paper and foil, but remember that foil can be eaten away by the acid in the fruits if left in direct contact, so be sure not to use foil basins for your puddings. Don't worry about leftover mincemeat, it can always be used for filling baked apples or mincemeat cake. Have a look at the Leftovers chapter for wonderful Mincemeat Flapjacks (page 171). Also featured in this chapter are a couple of puddings and cakes that freeze especially well. There are of course many other dishes throughout the book that freeze well and I have indicated these when appropriate.

One of the things that I really love to do in the weeks leading up to Christmas is to make several batches of Shortbread (page 27) – a prettily wrapped tin of home-made shortbread is one of the best possible presents to give to friends and family in the run-up to December 25th.

Whilst you are busy doing all this preparation, be sure to fill your house with some seasonal aroma – simply slice some oranges, lay them on a baking tray and gently dry then in the simmering oven. In my oven it takes about 8 hours, but as Agas vary from household to household be sure to keep an eye on them to make sure that they don't blacken. When dried they can then be tied together with cinnamon sticks or displayed in bowls.

There is, of course, one danger to this well thought through preparation; you can all too easily be lulled into a false sense of security and become complacent about all that still has to be done.
I'm afraid the sad truth is that when it comes to Christmas you can never really fully relax…!

Granny's Christmas Pudding

This recipe has been taken from my second book *The Traditional Aga Party Book* and I think it's the best recipe for Christmas pudding that I have ever tried. It has always proved hugely popular at my demonstrations around the country, even with those who, at first, are adamant that they don't like Christmas pudding! Traditionally, puddings are made on the first Sunday of Advent, also known as 'Stir-up Sunday' when everyone is at home to have a stir and a wish. I usually make mine a month or so earlier than this, but we all still enjoy the tradition.

250g/9oz suet (I use 'vegetable suet', suitable for vegetarians)
350g/12oz Demerara sugar
500g /1lb 2oz sultanas
500g/1lb 2oz currants
500g/1lb 2oz raisins
1 cooking apple, peeled and grated
15g/$\frac{1}{2}$oz ground mixed spice
15g/$\frac{1}{2}$oz ground ginger
Pinch salt
Grated rind and juice 1 lemon
Grated rind and juice 1 orange
300ml/$\frac{1}{2}$ pint Guinness
300ml/$\frac{1}{2}$ pint water
60ml/2 fl oz brandy
30ml/1 fl oz sherry
30ml/1 fl oz rum
5 eggs, beaten
350g/12oz fresh breadcrumbs

Put all the ingredients except the eggs and the breadcrumbs in a large mixing bowl and mix thoroughly. Cover and leave to stand somewhere cool for 3 to 4 days, stirring occasionally. When you are ready to cook the puddings, add the eggs and breadcrumbs to the soaked fruit mixture and stir thoroughly. Spoon the mixture into basins. Level the top and cover with a double layer circle of greaseproof paper. Then cover with a fitted lid, if using boilable plastic basins, or a double layer of foil, if using a traditional basin.

Stand each pudding on a trivet, or an old plate and place on the base of a saucepan. (It is useful to stand the basin in a strap of foil, so it can be easily lifted from the hot pan.) Pour in enough water to come 5cm/2" up the side of the pudding basin. Cover the pan with a lid and bring to the boil. Move to the simmering plate and simmer for 25-30 minutes. (You may need to pull the pan half off the plate to keep to a simmer.) Move the puddings to the simmering oven and leave to cook for 11 or 12 hours. Remove from the oven and allow to completely cool. When cold, replace the greaseproof paper and foil with fresh pieces and then store the puddings somewhere cool.

On Christmas Day, place the pudding directly in the simmering oven for 1-2 hours. Cool for 10 minutes before turning out onto a warm serving plate.

**Makes either 2 large (2 litre/3 pint) puddings or
3 medium (1 litre/2 pint) puddings**

A Light Christmas Pudding

This is a deliciously light alternative to the more traditional dark and heavily fruited Christmas pudding. It's a recipe that doesn't contain a large quantity of dried fruits, so won't keep as long as the classic pudding. However, it will keep in the fridge for 3 or 4 days and can be frozen, which makes it perfect as a last minute pudding.

175g/6oz butter, softened
175g/6oz caster sugar
Grated rind 2 oranges
3 eggs, beaten
175g/6oz self-raising flour
1 level teaspoon ground cinnamon
75g/3oz ready-to-eat prunes, chopped
75g/3oz ready-to-eat apricots, chopped
75g/3oz ready-to-eat figs, chopped
75g/3oz Lexia or large juicy raisins,
    chopped

Put the butter and sugar in a bowl and cream together until light and fluffy. Beat in the grated orange rind. Gradually beat in the eggs, adding a little flour with each addition to help the egg mix in. When all the egg has been added, add the cinnamon to the flour and fold into the creamed mixture. Fold in the chopped fruits.

Spoon the mixture into a buttered 1.4 litre/ $2^{1}/_{2}$ pint pudding basin.

Cover the top either with a fitted lid if using a boilable plastic basin, or cover the pudding with greaseproof paper and foil. Put a trivet or an old saucer into the bottom of a saucepan and put in the pudding. (It is useful to stand the basin in a strap of foil so it can be easily lifted from the hot pan).

Add enough water to the saucepan to come 5cm/2" up the side of the saucepan. Cover the pan with a lid. Bring the water to the boil and then simmer on the simmering plate for 30 minutes. Move the saucepan to the simmering oven and cook for 5-6 hours. At this point the pudding can be served, or cooled and stored in the fridge, or frozen. If freezing, remove from the freezer and thaw in a cool place overnight, and then proceed as for reheating. To reheat, place the pudding directly in the simmering oven for 1-2 hours. Cool for 10 minutes before turning out onto a warmed serving plate.

Serves 8–10

Marzipan

You can buy very good quality marzipan from the supermarket, which is easy to use, though it doesn't have the wonderful flavour and texture of homemade. The added bonus of making marzipan by hand (using a food processor will make it too oily) is that your hands will be beautifully soothed and smoothed by the almond oil!

300g/10$\frac{1}{2}$oz ground almonds
225g/8oz icing sugar, sieved
225g/8oz caster sugar
1 whole egg and 2 egg yolks, beaten together
1 teaspoon lemon juice
$\frac{1}{2}$ teaspoon vanilla essence

Mix the almonds and the sugars together in a mixing bowl. Add the remaining ingredients and mix to a stiff paste. (The easiest way of doing this is to use your hands.) Turn the paste onto a work surface and knead until well mixed and crack free. If the marzipan feels a little sticky add a little icing sugar to the surface. Unwrap the cake and place it on a cake board or plate. The cake will be level on the top so there is no need to turn the cake upside down or trim the top. Roll the marzipan into a circle to fit over the top and sides of the cake and brush the top and sides with warm apricot jam. Lift the marzipan onto a rolling pin and carefully lay over the cake. Using your hands, carefully stroke the marzipan onto the top and sides of the cake, starting in the middle of the top and working outwards and down the sides. Press and smooth the marzipan to fit the cake. Trim any excess from the base.

Allow the marzipan to dry for 3-4 days before icing (unless you are doing this at the last minute and will be eating the cake in the next day or two).

Royal Icing

Royal icing can either be used as a smooth surface icing and for piping, or applied 'roughly' with a palette knife to create a snow scene.

2 egg whites
450g/1lb icing sugar, sieved
$\frac{1}{2}$ teaspoon lemon juice
2-3 drops glycerine (optional), to keep the icing softer

Beat the egg whites until foamy, but not white. Gradually beat in the icing sugar, lemon juice and glycerine. Continue beating in the sugar until the icing is snowy white, smooth, and stands in stiff peaks when the spoon is lifted from the bowl. If it is too stiff add more lemon juice, or if too soft, more icing sugar. Add a few drops of colouring at this stage if desired. Cover tightly with clingfilm and allow to stand for an hour or two or even overnight, this allows the bubbles to disperse, which is especially beneficial if you want a smooth icing.

Brush any excess icing sugar from the marzipan on the cake and apply the icing with a palette knife. If the icing begins to stick to the knife, just dip the blade in warm water. Keep any extra icing in the bowl and keep covered at all times to prevent the icing drying out.

This quantity is sufficient to cover the top and sides of a 23cm/9" round cake.

Christmas Cake

A traditional rich fruit cake with the slightly unusual but succulent addition of apricots and figs. You can of course add any dried fruits that you like. If this is the first time you have baked a rich fruit cake in your Aga, I suggest that you bake it during the day and make a note on the recipe for future reference of how long it takes to cook. Don't be surprised by the length of the cooking time, and remember that the tin does not need wrapping on the outside.

1 kg/2lb 2oz dried fruits, such as raisins,
   sultanas, mixed peel and cherries
100g/3$\frac{1}{2}$oz dried apricots, chopped
100g/3$\frac{1}{2}$oz dried figs, chopped
75g/2$\frac{3}{4}$oz blanched almonds, chopped
150ml/5fl oz sherry
Finely grated rind and juice 1 orange
250g/9oz butter, softened
175g/6oz soft brown sugar
5 eggs, beaten
300g/10$\frac{1}{2}$oz plain flour
75g/2$\frac{3}{4}$oz self raising flour
3 level teaspoons mixed spice
1 level teaspoon ground cinnamon
1 tablespoon golden syrup and
   1 tablespoon fine-cut orange marmalade

In a large non-metallic bowl, put the dried fruits, apricots, figs, almonds, sherry, orange rind and juice. Mix well, cover and leave to stand for 24 hours.

Line the inside of a 20cm/8" deep round cake tin. Cream the butter and sugar together until light and fluffy. Gradually beat in the eggs, alternating with a little flour, to prevent the mixture curdling. Fold in the remaining flour and spices. Gently fold in the golden syrup and the marmalade and then the soaked fruit mixture. Spoon the mixture into the prepared tin and level the top. Place the oven shelf on the floor of the simmering oven and put in the cake. Bake for 9-12 hours (some 'cool' simmering ovens may take up to 24 hours) until the top of the cake is evenly pale golden, the cake has shrunk from the sides of the tin, and a skewer inserted in the middle comes out clean. Allow to completely cool in the tin. Turn out when cold and wrap the cake in greaseproof paper and foil. Store somewhere cool until ready to marzipan and ice the cake (see page 15).

Christmas Fruit and Nut Cake

This is not as heavily fruited as the traditional Christmas Cake on page 17. However, the extra mix of nuts gives it a delicious crunch. It will keep well but can also be made a day or two before eating.

250g/9oz raisins
350g/12oz sultanas
200g/7oz glace cherries, rinsed and halved
50g/2 oz candied peel, finely chopped
100g/3$\frac{1}{2}$oz pecans
100g/3$\frac{1}{2}$oz hazelnuts
100g/3$\frac{1}{2}$oz shelled pistachios
Grated rind and juice 1 lemon
4 tablespoons brandy or sherry
325g/11oz plain flour
2 teaspoons ground allspice
75g/2$\frac{1}{2}$oz ground almonds
250g/9oz soft brown sugar
250g/9oz butter, softened
2 tablespoons treacle
5 eggs, beaten

Put the dried fruits, peel, nuts, lemon rind, juice and the brandy or sherry together in a mixing bowl. Mix well, cover and leave to stand overnight.

Mix the flour, spices and ground almonds together. Cream together the butter and the sugar until light and fluffy. Gradually beat in the eggs, adding a little flour mixture between each addition. Beat in the treacle and then fold in the remaining flour mixture. Finally, add the soaked fruit and nuts, stirring gently until all are evenly mixed.

Spoon the mixture into a lined 23cm/9" deep cake tin. Put the shelf on the floor of the simmering oven and put in the cake. Bake for 8-12 hours, or until the cake has shrunk from the sides of the tin and a skewer inserted in the middle comes out clean. Cool the cake in the tin. When cold, remove from the tin and wrap in greaseproof paper and then foil. The cake can be served either without decoration or covered with marzipan and icing (see page 15).

Makes 1 x 23cm/9" round cake

Chocolate Cake

This cake is a great favourite in my family, and is a really good alternative for those who do not like traditional Christmas cake. I first started making and freezing this when we found ourselves away in London supporting chorister sons on Christmas Eve, arriving home late in the West Country on Christmas Day. We developed the habit then of tea and chocolate cake in front of the fire whilst opening a few presents, Boxing Day becoming our day for stockings and traditional Christmas fare. Be reassured that truffles, golden pennies and tartan ribbon freeze well!

100g/3$\frac{1}{2}$oz plain chocolate
4 eggs, separated
175g/6oz butter, softened
175g/6oz soft brown sugar
150g/5$\frac{1}{2}$oz self-raising flour
25g/1oz cocoa powder
1 teaspoon vanilla extract
3 tablespoons boiling water

For the filling and covering
300ml/$\frac{1}{2}$ pint double cream
175g/6oz plain chocolate

For the decoration
12 gold or silver covered chocolate
   pennies
12 cocoa-dusted truffles
Tartan ribbon to tie round the cake

Grease and base-line two 23cm/9" sandwich cake tins.

Put the chocolate in a basin and stand at the back of the Aga to melt. Put the egg whites in a mixer bowl and whisk until soft peaks form. Put the butter and sugar in a mixing bowl and cream until light and fluffy. Beat in the egg yolks and the vanilla extract. Fold in the flour and cocoa. Fold in the melted chocolate and then slowly add the hot water. When everything has evenly mixed, lightly beat in 1 tablespoon of the whisked egg white and then gently fold in the remaining egg white.

Divide the mixture between the two tins and level the surface. Place in the oven to bake; for a two-oven Aga put the shelf on the floor of the roasting oven. Put in the cakes and slide in the cold shelf on the second set of runners from the bottom of the oven. For a three- or four-oven Aga; put the shelf on the bottom set of runners of the baking oven and put in the cakes.

The cakes will take 20-25 minutes. They are cooked when they become firm to the touch when lightly pressed in the middle, and have slightly shrunk from the sides of the tin. Cool for 5 minutes in the tin and then turn out onto a cooling rack until cold.

Put the chocolate for the covering in a roomy basin on the back of the Aga until melted. Allow the cream to warm to room temperature. To assemble the cake, put one cake upside down on the serving plate, or a sheet of foil if freezing. Add the cream to the melted chocolate and beat well. The mixture will start to thicken and it will become firm when cold. Spread some of the chocolate cream onto the inverted cake and lay the other half on top.

Use the remaining mixture to cover the top and sides of the cake using a table knife. Decorate the top, alternating with truffles and foil-covered pennies standing upright. Tie the ribbon round the cake. Allow to set for an hour before serving or freezing.

Mince Pies

I have never actually counted the number of mince pies that I make over the Christmas period. I really should one day. It probably runs into the hundreds! It's not only family and friends that devour them but also all those who come along to my many Christmas Aga demonstrations. As you can imagine, I have pretty much perfected the art of making mince pies in advance. I make my mince pies in mini muffin tins. You can use any size tin that you like, but to my mind these are the perfect bite-sized morsels. The tins may seem expensive, but they do have a variety of uses (they are perfect for making nibbles for drinks parties for example). You will need four one-dozen tins. Two tins will fit neatly on the floor of the roasting oven at a time. You can make your own pastry for the mince pies but for speed and full-proof results I tend to use supermarket Dessert Short Crust pastry. I use a star cutter shape for the lids of the pies – they look attractive and the little air gaps mean there is no need to spend time sealing the tops. The mince pies are frozen uncooked – freshly baked pastry always tastes best, and the raw pastry pies tend not to get broken so easily in the freezer.

2 x 375g packs of dessert short crust pastry
1 x 450g jar homemade mincemeat (see following recipes)

Roll one pack of pastry out and cut out 24 stars. Use the remaining pastry to cut circles for the base of the pies. Carefully line each muffin mould with a pastry circle. Spoon one teaspoon of mincemeat into each pastry case. Top with a star of pastry.

If making the mince pies in advance, put the trays of mince pies in the freezer. If you want to use the tins in the meantime, flip the mince pies out carefully, using a round bladed knife, and store them in a plastic box until needed.

To bake, return the pies to the tins, if they have been stored and, whether freshly made or frozen, put the tins directly on the floor of the roasting oven and bake for 8-10 minutes for freshly-made pies or 12-15 minutes for frozen. The dessert pastry can brown very easily, so keep an eye on them – when baked they should be a pale golden colour. Leave in the tin for 2-3 minutes before removing and serve warm, dusted with icing sugar.

Makes 24 mini mince pies

Apricot Mincemeat

My favourite mincemeat, slightly adapted over the years. It's a great favourite both at Aga demonstrations and also with friends who receive jars at Christmas time.

225g/8oz ready-to-eat apricots, finely chopped
Grated rind and juice of 1 orange
1kg/2lb 4oz currants, raisins and sultanas, mixed
4 tablespoons fine-cut orange marmalade
450g/1lb unrefined golden caster sugar
225g/8oz shredded suet (I use the vegetable suet for vegetarian mincemeat)
1$\frac{1}{2}$ teaspoons mixed spice
$\frac{1}{2}$ teaspoon freshly grated nutmeg
200ml/7fl oz brandy

Put all the ingredients into a large mixing bowl. Mix together thoroughly. Cover and leave to steep for 24 hours. When ready to use, drain the apricots through a colander, rinse and dry off. Put them in a roomy mixing bowl and add all the remaining ingredients. Mix together thoroughly. Cover and leave to steep for 24 hours.

Spoon the mincemeat into clean, sterile jars. Cover with a wax disc and a jar lid (the mincemeat will dry out if cellophane lids are used). Label and store in a dark, cool place.

Fills 4 x 450g/1lb jars

Sugar-free Mincemeat

This is a perfect recipe for those who are diabetic or just looking to reduce their refined sugar intake. Because no additional sugar is added to the fruits, the mincemeat needs to be preserved by heating the fruit and allowing it to become coated with the fat from the suet. The finished mincemeat will keep well if placed in a cool, dark cupboard.

450g/1lb cooking apple, peeled, cored and
   grated
250g/9oz shredded suet
350g/12oz raisins
350g/12oz currants
350g/12oz sultanas
Grated rind and juice 2 oranges
Grated rind and juice 2 lemons
50g/2oz blanched almonds, slivered
4 teaspoons mixed spice
1 teaspoon ground cinnamon
1 teaspoon freshly grated nutmeg
100ml/3$\frac{1}{2}$fl oz brandy

Put all the ingredients, except the brandy, in a large bowl (suitable for the simmering oven) and mix well. Cover and leave to stand for 12 hours and then mix again. Re-cover and stand for another 12 hours.

Cover the bowl with foil. Place the shelf on the bottom of the simmering oven and put in the bowl of mincemeat. Leave for 4-5 hours. Remove from the oven and stir well. Allow the mixture to cool and then add the brandy. Stir well. When the mincemeat is cold, spoon into clean, sterile jars. Cover with wax discs and seal with lids. Label and store in a cool dark place.

Makes about 2.25kg/5lb

Cranberry Mincemeat

A vibrantly colourful mincemeat that needs to be heated in order to develop a velvety texture and to ensure that it keeps well.

450g/1lb fresh cranberries, washed, dried and picked over
200g/7oz dried cranberries
600g/1¼lb raisins
600g/1¼lb sultanas
400g/14oz candied peel, finely chopped
250g/9oz shredded vegetable suet
2 medium cooking apples, peeled and grated
600g/1¼lb soft brown sugar
100g/3½oz almonds, thinly sliced
Grated rind and juice 4 oranges
1 teaspoon ground cinnamon
6 teaspoons mixed spice
1 teaspoon freshly grated nutmeg
150ml/¼ pint brandy

In a large bowl (suitable for the simmering oven), mix together all the ingredients, except the brandy. Stir very well. Cover and leave to blend overnight.

Cover with foil and put the bowl in the simmering oven for 2-3 hours. Remove from the oven and stir again very well. Stir in the brandy and leave to go completely cold before packing into sterile jars. Seal and label the jars.

Makes about 4 large jars

Shortbread

Christmas has become the traditional time for buying or making shortbread.
It is easy to make and, when packed in pretty tins, makes a lovely gift.

110g/4oz butter
110g/4oz plain white flour
50g/2oz rice flour
50g/2oz caster sugar

Put all the ingredients into a mixing bowl. Rub in the butter until the mixture resembles breadcrumbs and carry on mixing until the butter warms through and the mixture comes together. Knead lightly. Divide the dough into two equal portions and roll out to two rounds – 20cm/8" in diameter and about 5 mm/ $1/4$" thick. I find this easiest to do on a piece of Bake-O-Glide. Pinch round the outer edges of the circles.

Invert a glass tumbler with a rim about $7^1/2$ cm/3" diameter into the middle of each shortbread round and cut round the tumbler, thus cutting a circle from the middle of the dough. Then cut 8 'tails' from the inside circle to the edge.
The inner circle not only looks attractive, but also prevents points of shortbread becoming too crisp during baking.
Slide the shortbreads onto a baking tray.

For a two-oven Aga; put the baking tray on the bottom set of runners of the roasting oven. Place the cold shelf on the second set of runners from the bottom of the oven. Bake for 20 minutes. For a three- or four-oven Aga; hang the tray on the bottom set of runners of the baking oven and bake the shortbread for 20-25 minutes.

The shortbread should be a very pale golden colour and look dry when cooked. Dredge with caster sugar whilst still warm.

Makes 2 rounds

Meringue Roulade
with Christmas Fruit Ice-Cream & Marsala Custard

A wonderfully indulgent seasonal pudding. The roulade needs to have at least 24 hours in the freezer and then be moved to the fridge 2 hours before serving. The Marsala Custard can be made up to 48 hours before using.

For the Meringue
5 egg whites
1 teaspoon cornflour
275g/9¼oz caster sugar
1 teaspoon white wine vinegar

For the Christmas Fruit Ice-Cream
1 litre/1¾ pints good quality ice cream
50g/2oz sultanas
2 tablespoons Marsala
75g/3oz orange candied peel, chopped
50g/2oz glace cherries, chopped

For the Marsala Custard
4 tablespoons Marsala
5 egg yolks
110g/4oz caster sugar
½ teaspoon ground cinnamon
½ teaspoon cornflour
600ml/1 pint milk

Firstly, make the fruit mixture for the ice cream. Put the sultanas and the Marsala into a basin and add the cherries and orange peel. Cover and leave to soak overnight.

Next, make the meringue. Line a large baking tray with a sheet of Bake-O-Glide. Mix together the caster sugar and the cornflour. Whisk the egg whites until thick and fluffy and keeping the whisk going, whisk in the sugar mixture one teaspoonful at a time. Lastly, whisk in the wine vinegar. Carefully spread the meringue into the lined tin.

Hang the tin on the bottom set of runners of the roasting oven and slide in the cold shelf onto the second set of runners from the top of the roasting oven. Cook for 10 minutes and then move the meringue to the simmering oven for 45 minutes. When ready, the meringue should be a very pale golden, and dry on the surface. Remove from the oven and leave to cool.

When ready to roll the roulade, remove the ice cream from the freezer and mix in the macerated fruits. Turn the cold meringue out onto a plain sheet of Bake-O-Glide. Very gently, spread the ice cream over the meringue. With the help of the Bake-O-Glide, roll the meringue into a roulade, making sure the longest side is nearest to you as you roll. Freeze until firm.

Now make the custard. Beat together the egg yolks, sugar, cinnamon and cornflour in a basin. Heat the milk until almost boiling and then whisk onto the egg mixture. Pour the egg mixture into the saucepan and stand on the simmering plate and whisk gently, until the custard thickens. Stir or whisk constantly, to prevent the custard curdling. When the custard is thick enough to coat the back of a wooden spoon, remove it from the heat and stir in the Marsala. Taste and adjust the amount of alcohol. Pour the custard into a jug or plastic box and chill. This sauce can be made up to 48 hours before you need it.

To serve, pour some of the Marsala custard onto a plate and place two thin slices of roulade on top.

Serves 8

Christmas Eve

Christmas Eve can be both an exciting and an exhausting day. The last minute preparations always seem to take just that little bit longer than you had anticipated. However, if you have cooked some of the recipes suggested in Cooking in Advance (page 10) and now follow on with the recipes in this section, it should leave you feeling reasonably prepared for the big day. Try to set yourself, and everyone else around you, a time when all the preparations should be finished. For me, this is early evening; long enough to relax before setting out to Midnight Mass.

By now you will have planned your menu, so keep the list of ingredients handy, and make sure you have all the items assembled and out of the freezer. Keep a wary eye out for anyone who attempts to eat in advance the food prepared for tomorrow!

If you have not done so already, today is the day you can bake a gammon (page 39), make stuffings (pages 32–34) and prepare sauces (pages 35–36) and vegetables.

Preparing vegetables for roasting saves so much time. Once the vegetables are cold, cover with foil or clingfilm and store somewhere cool. On Christmas Day just place them straight in the oven to roast.

One other thing to do today is make stock (page 37) from the turkey giblets (you should have asked your butcher to keep them for you).

In my family, trifle (page 40) is a favourite pudding for Christmas day and is perfect for those who don't like the heavier Christmas pudding so beloved of most British households. It's fairly quick to make on Christmas Eve and needs little final decoration on the day.

When all the cooking has finally been done on Christmas Eve, I would strongly recommend that you turn up your Aga just a tweak so that it has a little extra core heat to cope with all the cooking that will be required of it on Christmas day. This is especially important for those with mains gas Agas, who will need to compensate for the reduced gas pressure that will be available as the entire country fires up its fuel for the biggest meal of the year.

Stuffings

Traditionally, stuffing is used to moisten and flavour meat and can be cooked within the meat or separately. It is not recommended that you stuff the cavity of turkey or chicken, but do put some stuffing in the neck end. Alternatively, cook the stuffing shaped as balls. Place on a baking tray lined with Bake-O-Glide in the roasting oven on the third set of runners for 30 minutes.

Sage and Onion Stuffing

A traditional stuffing for turkey, chicken or goose.

15g/$\frac{1}{2}$oz butter
1 large onion, peeled and finely chopped
1 kg/2$\frac{1}{4}$lb fresh sausage meat
225g/8oz streaky bacon, rind removed and chopped
1 tablespoon sage, finely chopped
Salt and pepper

Heat the butter in a frying pan and cook the onion until soft but not brown. Cool. Put the sausage meat and bacon into a large bowl and mix well. Add the onion, sage and a seasoning of salt and pepper. Mix very well together (I find the easiest way of doing this is with my hands). Use this to stuff the neck end of a bird, or to form into stuffing balls (see introduction text, above). This can be frozen for up to one month.

Forcemeat Stuffing

A traditional stuffing for goose, though it is also an excellent all-rounder

1 small onion, peeled and finely chopped
Liver from the bird, if available, chopped
Rind and juice 1 orange, finely grated
225g/8oz sausage meat
2 teaspoons chopped thyme leaves
3 tablespoons chopped fresh parsley
50g/2oz fresh breadcrumbs
Salt and pepper
1 egg, beaten

Place all the ingredients except the egg in a mixing bowl. Mix together and then add enough egg to bind the stuffing together. Use to stuff the neck end of a bird or to form into stuffing balls (see introduction text, above). This stuffing can be frozen for up to one month.

Fruit Stuffing

This stuffing is good with rich meats such as goose, duck and pork.

110g/4oz stoned prunes, chopped
110g/4oz dried apricots, chopped
85ml/3fl oz port
2 eating apples, cored and chopped
1 small onion, peeled and finely chopped
$\frac{1}{2}$ teaspoon ground cinnamon
A little grated nutmeg
50g/2oz fresh breadcrumbs
Salt and pepper

Put the chopped prunes and apricots in a basin and pour over the port. Cover and leave to soak for several hours or overnight. Place all the remaining ingredients in a mixing bowl. Add the soaked fruits and mix to bind together. Either use to stuff the cavity of a goose, or cook separately in a dish.

Chestnut Stuffing

Chestnuts make a rich and moist stuffing for turkey. You can cook your own in the roasting oven, but do remember to slit them before putting in the oven or else they will explode! The vacuum-packed ones make an excellent and easy alternative.

2 tablespoons olive oil
1 onion, peeled and finely chopped
450g/1lb sausage meat
100g/3$\frac{1}{2}$oz ready-to-eat prunes, chopped
400g/14oz cooked chestnuts, chopped
2 tablespoons chopped fresh parsley
Salt and pepper

Heat one tablespoon of the olive oil in a frying pan and sauté the onion until soft but not brown. Cool. Put the remaining ingredients, except the remaining olive oil, in a mixing bowl. Add the cooled onion and mix well. Divide the mixture into 24 portions and roll into balls. Pour the remaining olive oil into your hand and roll each stuffing ball to lightly coat with oil. Place on a baking tray lined with Bake-O-Glide. Bake for 30-35 minutes. These stuffing balls can be frozen for up to one month.

Potato and Apple Stuffing

This is an excellent stuffing, suitable for those who cannot tolerate gluten.
It is best cooked in the neck of the turkey or goose for added flavour.

1 kg/2¼lb potatoes, peeled
50g/2oz butter
2 onions, peeled and finely chopped
2 large cooking apples, peeled and
    chopped
Grated rind and juice 1 lemon
1 tablespoon chopped fresh thyme leaves
Salt and pepper

Put the potatoes in a saucepan, add
2.5cm/1" water, cover and bring to the
boil. Boil for 2-3 minutes, drain the water
away and put the covered pan in the
simmering oven for 40-50 minutes, until
the potatoes are soft. Ensure the potatoes
are drained well and then mash.

Melt the butter in a pan and sauté the
onion until soft, but not brown. Add the
apples, cover with a lid and cook until the
apples are fluffy, about 4-5 minutes. Stir in
the lemon rind and juice and the thyme.
Combine the apple mixture and the mash
potato. Mix well and season with salt and
pepper. Chill before using. Place on a
baking tray lined with Bake-O-Glide.
Bake for 30-35 minutes.

Bread Sauce

This is a rich and very slightly spicy sauce that can be made on Christmas Eve and warmed through on the day.

1 large onion, peeled
6-8 cloves
1 bay leaf
6 whole peppercorns
600ml/1 pint whole milk
110g/4oz fresh breadcrumbs
50g/2oz butter, diced
1-2 tablespoons single cream
Salt

Stick the cloves into the onion and place in a milk pan. Add the bay leaf and the peppercorns. Pour in the milk. Stand on the simmering plate and bring slowly to the boil. Remove from the heat and stand at the back of the Aga for 30 minutes to allow the flavours to infuse.

Strain the milk through a sieve and rinse out the pan. Return the infused milk to the pan and heat gently. Add the breadcrumbs and the butter to the warm milk and stir well until the butter has melted. Add the cream and adjust the seasoning.

Pour into a serving dish and cover with foil to keep warm either on the back of the Aga, or in the warming oven, or serve immediately. If you have prepared it the day before using, cool and place in a box in the fridge. Reheat in the warming oven.

Serves 8

Horseradish Sauce

This is a wonderfully creamy horseradish sauce. It will keep for a day or two in the fridge where it will improve in flavour.

150ml/5fl oz double cream
1-2 tablespoons grated fresh horseradish,
    depending upon taste
2 teaspoons white wine vinegar
Salt and pepper

Lightly whip the cream and then fold in the remaining ingredients. Chill for 2-3 hours to allow the flavours to develop.

The sauce is best served at room temperature.

Cranberry Sauce

Cranberries are imported from America. When they first came here all the recipes we seemed to use were American. I found that the sauce tended to be too sweet in the American versions, so I have created a recipe for my own taste. The use of the orange rind and juice helps to reduce the amount of sugar needed.

250g/9oz cranberries
75g/3oz caster sugar
Grated rind and juice 1 orange

Pick over the cranberries and remove stalks and any bruised or soft berries. Wash the remaining cranberries and put them in a saucepan. Add the sugar and the grated rind and juice of the orange. Cover with a lid. Stand the pan on the simmering plate and cook gently – you may hear the berries bursting. When all the berries are cooked (after about 5 minutes) remove from the heat. Stir through. Serve immediately, or cool and keep in a box in the fridge for up to 3 or 4 days. Serve warm or cold. This will freeze well for up to one month.

Apple Sauce

A traditional sauce served with roast pork, a favourite of many at Christmas time, that adds a slight cut to the fattiness of the meat. It will keep well in the fridge for several days.

450g/1lb cooking apples, peeled,
    quartered and roughly chopped
Finely grated rind and juice of ½ lemon
2 teaspoons sugar
2 tablespoons water
15g/½oz butter

Place the prepared apples in a saucepan and add the lemon juice, rind and the water. Cover with a lid and stand on the simmering plate. Cook gently until the apples are soft (the length of time will depend upon the variety of apple). When the apple is soft, beat well with a wooden spoon or potato masher. Add the sugar and the butter. Mix in well. Taste and add more sugar if needed. Serve hot or cold.

Giblet Stock

A good stock, perfect for enriching your Christmas Day gravy. Be sure to ask your butcher to set aside the giblets for you. You should use all of the giblets except the liver.

Giblets from your turkey
A selection of flavouring vegetables (such as onions, carrots, celery), washed and chopped, but not necessarily peeled
A few peppercorns
1 bouquet garni

Place the giblets into a large saucepan. Add the vegetables, the peppercorns and the bouquet garni. Cover with cold water and put a lid onto the saucepan. Place on the boiling plate and bring to the boil. Transfer to the simmering oven for 2-3 hours. Remove the saucepan from the oven, cool and skim off excess fat. Strain through a sieve and either store in the fridge for immediate use, or freeze.

Traditional
Glazed Gammon

I love home-cooked ham at Christmas. It is always so useful for eking out meals for unexpected guests. Once you have cooked a gammon at home you won't be satisfied with the bought variety. If possible, find a butcher who cures his own gammons and ask him how long he thinks the joint needs to soak in order to remove excess salts before cooking.

Soak the joint in cold water for 2-3 hours. Drain. Put a trivet or old plate in the base of a saucepan large enough to take the joint. Pour in enough water, cider or apple juice, to come no more than 5cm/2" up the side of the pan. Cover with a lid.

Stand on the simmering plate and slowly bring to the boil. Simmer for 30 minutes and then move to the simmering oven (for weights and cooking times, see 'Gammon Cooking Times' in the Appendix on page 180).

Remove the pan from the oven and lift the gammon from the pan. When cool enough to handle, strip off the skin and score a diamond pattern on the fat. Spread the fat with mustard and stud the centre of each diamond with a clove. Press Demerara sugar all over the mustard.

Stand the ham on a baking tray lined with Bake-O-Glide. Hang the tray on the second set of runners from the bottom of the roasting oven and allow a crust and glaze to form for 20-30 minutes, keeping an eye on it so that it doesn't burn. Allow it to rest for 20-30 minutes before carving, if serving hot, otherwise allow it to cool.

If you choose a joint on the bone, the chances are that you won't have a saucepan large enough to cook it in following this method. In which case, put the rack on its lowest setting, in the large Aga roasting tin. Place the soaked joint on the rack and pour in enough water to come just around the meat. Cover as tightly with foil as possible, remembering that the foil will tear if put on the runners. Put the tin on the floor of the roasting oven and cook for 1 hour before moving to the simmering oven for the appropriate time (see appendix on page 180).

When the ham is cold, wrap it in greaseproof paper – not foil or clingfilm – and keep in the fridge or somewhere cool. It will keep well for at least a week.

Traditional Trifle

This trifle is often requested in my house as an alternative to Christmas pudding. It's easy to make and improves in flavour if made at least 24 hours before eating.

2 boxes trifle sponges
200g/7oz best quality raspberry jam
150ml/¼ pint sweet sherry or Marsala
150ml/¼ pint apple juice
100g/3½oz (about 28) amaretti or ratafia
    biscuits
2 medium bananas
300ml/½ pint single cream
300ml/½ pint milk
1 vanilla pod
4 eggs
75g/3oz caster sugar
2 level teaspoons cornflour
300ml/½ pint double cream, whipped
Glacé cherries and chopped nuts, to
    decorate

Separate the trifle sponges and cut in half. Spread with jam and sandwich together. Cut each sponge in half and lay them in the serving dish.

Mix together the sherry and the apple juice and pour over the sponges. Roughly crumble over the amaretti biscuits. Peel and slice the bananas and lay on top of the amaretti. Cover and set aside.

Pour the single cream and the milk into a saucepan and add the vanilla pod. Stand on the simmering plate and allow to slowly come to the boil. Remove from the heat and leave to cool and infuse for 10 minutes. Slit the pod in half lengthways and scrape the seeds into the cream.

In a basin, beat together the eggs, caster sugar and the cornflour. When smooth, slowly beat in the infused cream. Mix well and then return the mixture to the saucepan. Stand the saucepan on the simmering plate and stir with a small whisk or a wooden spoon continuously, until the custard thickens enough to coat the back of a wooden spoon. (Do not allow the mixture to boil.) Cover tightly with clingfilm and allow to cool. Pour the custard over the trifle and leave until cold. Whip the double cream until it is just holding its shape and carefully spoon over the top of the trifle. Decorate with glacé cherries and chopped nuts.

Brandy Butter

Personally, I prefer brandy sauce to brandy butter, but this was a great favourite of my Father's, and I remember making this recipe on Christmas Eve when I was quite young. I love it with mince pies. If preferred, you can replace the brandy with rum.

225g/8oz unsalted butter, at room
  temperature
225g/8oz caster sugar
Finely grated rind 1 orange
4-6 tablespoons brandy

Cream together the butter and the sugar until very light and fluffy. Beat in the orange rind and then slowly beat in the brandy, adding as much as is needed to give quite a strong brandy flavour. Spoon into a serving dish, or storage box and chill well. Serve chilled.

Sherry Sauce

This creamy sauce is remarkably light to eat. It is a popular accompaniment to Christmas pudding, especially for those who prefer something lighter than brandy butter. If preferred, you can replace the sherry with brandy.

600ml/1 pint single cream
50g/2oz butter
50g/2oz flour
50g/2oz caster sugar
6 tablespoons sweet sherry

Pour the cream into a milk pan. Add the flour and the butter. Stand the pan on the simmering plate and whisk the mixture continuously until the sauce has thickened. Bubble gently for 2-3 minutes. Remove from the heat and stir in the sherry. If the sauce is to be served immediately, whisk in the sugar and pour into a warm serving jug. If you are not serving immediately, you can prevent a skin forming by scattering the caster sugar over the surface of the sauce. Whisk the sugar into the sauce just before serving.

Serves 8-10

Traditional Trifle

Trifle is a centuries-old dessert which makes
a fine and much lighter alternative to
Christmas pudding at this time of year.
With its various layers, colours and toppings
it also always looks so very festive.

Traditional trifle, page 40

Christmas Day

Well the big day has arrived!

So, in order to try and bring some calm into what is inevitably a fairly frantic morning for the cook, I have included a fail-safe countdown for a traditional roast turkey lunch that I hope proves helpful. The turkey weight is 7.25kg/16 lb. If you are stuffing the bird, add on the weight of the stuffing, in this case about 1.5 kg/3 lb 5 oz. Following the countdown, the turkey will need fast-roasting for 3 hours – the times I have quoted are for serving lunch at 2 pm. Adjust the timings to suit your weight of turkey, cooking method and serving times. See Cooking the Turkey (page 47).

Just a little suggestion before you start; be sure to keep a bottle of Champagne in the fridge for the cook and those helping – it is all too easy to be forgotten in the Christmas rush!

Aga Christmas Day Countdown

9.00am
Move the turkey to a place in the kitchen where it can be left to come to room temperature. Stuff the turkey and put it in the roasting tin, lattice with bacon and put a butter paper or foil over the breast to prevent over browning.

10.00am
Put the turkey on the bottom set of runners of the roasting oven. Take the vegetables to be roasted from the fridge and leave to warm to room temperature. Do the same with the stuffing balls and bacon wraps.

12.30pm
Bring those vegetables to the boil that need to cook ready for mashing. Drain and put in the simmering oven. Make the Bread Sauce (page 35) and the Sherry Sauce (page 41), if you have not already done so. Cover tightly with clingfilm and stand at the back of the Aga to keep warm. Take the Cranberry Sauce (page 36) out of the fridge and put in a serving dish to allow it to warm to room temperature.

12.45pm
Put the vegetables to roast in the roasting oven. If the turkey is golden brown and there is room in the oven, put the vegetables on the top set of runners. Alternatively, put the tray on the floor of the roasting oven. Put the Christmas pudding directly in the simmering oven. Take the trifle out of the fridge and allow to warm to room temperature. Put plates and serving dishes to warm.

1.00pm
Check to see if the turkey has cooked through. When it has, remove from the oven and put onto a serving platter. Cover with foil and keep warm on the top or near the Aga. Move the roast vegetables to the bottom set of runners of the roasting oven and put in the tray of stuffing balls and bacon rolls. Make the gravy (page 50). Set aside. Fast boil the gravy just before serving.

1.40pm
Boil the sprouts and any other green vegetable. While the sprouts are cooking, mash any other vegetables and put into serving dishes. Toss the cooked and drained sprouts in butter. Put in a serving dish. All the roast vegetables can now be served and the stuffings and bacon rolls put onto a serving plate.

1.55pm
Take the pudding from the oven and leave to rest.

2.00pm(ish)
Call everyone to the table, pour the wine and relax (a bit)!

Cooking the Turkey

You have the choice of whether to roast the turkey slowly in the simmering oven or in the roasting oven by the medium or fast method. Obviously the first thing to consider is how much time you have and when you wish to eat. Here are a few pointers to help you decide which is the best method for you. The turkey needs to be taken out of the fridge at least an hour before roasting. Always remember to add on the weight of any stuffing to the weight of the bird. If you have a two-oven Aga you may prefer to use the simmering oven and free up the roasting oven for roasting the vegetables. Another thing to remember is that the turkey will need to rest for half an hour between coming out of the oven and being carved.

Preparing the turkey for the oven
Ask your butcher to remove the wishbone, this makes carving easier, though it's not essential. Stuff the neck end and fix the skin with a skewer. Do not stuff the cavity – with a bird heavily stuffed, there is a danger of it not cooking thoroughly. If you prefer, you can put an onion, lemon and some bay leaves in the cavity to add flavour.

Put the turkey in the large roasting tin. If liked, you can lattice some streaky bacon rashers over the breast and tops of the legs. This looks attractive and keeps those areas that are particularly prone to dryness, moist. Sometimes the flesh immediately under the bacon can develop a pink tinge, this is perfectly harmless. A little softened butter may be smeared over the exposed skin. Put a small piece of foil or a butter paper over the top of the turkey. Remove it half an hour before the turkey is cooked to allow the bacon to crisp. I don't like the idea of tenting foil

over my turkey to keep it moist because it can cause the meat to steam rather than roast – after all, the Aga ovens are renowned for the way they keep food moist. This also means there is no need to baste. Anyway, it's so difficult to remove a heavy turkey from the oven without being splashed by the fat!

All roasting times given are approximate and you must check that the turkey is cooked through. If in doubt, return the turkey to the oven for a further 30 minutes and then re-check (see page 49 on how to check that the bird is cooked).

Turkey roasting – fast method
Follow the instructions above for preparing your turkey for the oven.
For a turkey weighing 8-12Ibs/3.6-5.4kg:
Hang the roasting tin on the bottom set of runners of the roasting oven and roast for $1^3/_4$-2 hours.

For other weights see pages 178-179.

Turkey roasting – medium method
This is a useful method if you have a three- or four-oven Aga and have the use of a baking oven because it frees up the roasting oven for roast vegetables, but keeps the simmering oven free for the pudding and steamed and mashed vegetables.

For a turkey weighing 8-12Ibs/3.6-5.4kg:
Hang the roasting tin in the roasting oven and roast the turkey for one hour.
Then move the bottom set of runners of the baking oven for $1^1/_2$-$2^1/_2$ hours.
For other weights see pages 178-179.

Turkey roasting – slow method
For a turkey weighing 8-12Ibs/3.6-5.4kg:
Hang the roasting tin on the bottom set of runners of the roasting oven for one hour. This is essential to get the turkey up to 60C (140F) for safe cooking. Then move the turkey to the simmering oven for 3-5 hours.

For other weights see pages 178-179.

Testing if the turkey is cooked
There are various ways of checking if the turkey has cooked:

* You can use a thermometer inserted into the thickest part of the thigh through to the cavity, not touching any bone. The temperature should read 70-72C (158-160 F).

* Insert a skewer through the thickest part of the leg, the juices should run clear, not pink. If the juices are pink, return the turkey to the oven. (Sometimes you don't get much juice, so this is difficult.)

* I think the best method is to insert a sharp knife between the leg and the breast and look to see that the meat has cooked and the tip of the blade comes out hot. The joint should also be able to freely wiggle when moved.

When you are sure the turkey has cooked through, remove it from the oven and lift onto a warm serving platter. Cover the bird loosely with foil and stand either on the warming plate or on a trivet on top of the boiling plate lid. While the turkey rests all the juices will settle in the meat, making it juicier and easier to carve. This half hour should give you time to make the gravy and finish all the accompaniments cooking.

Gravy

For foolproof gravy you need a large balloon whisk and a flour shaker, these prevent lumps forming. Turkeys vary in the amount of fat and liquid there will be in the pan. If there is a substantial amount of fat then skim some off, but you will need a little to make a good sauce. Take the pan off the heat and shake a layer of flour over the base, whisk the flour in and gather all the sediments from the base of the tin. Repeat this two or three times and then gradually whisk in the giblet stock (see page 37).

Put the roasting tin on the simmering plate and continue to whisk, allowing the liquid to bubble and thicken. Add more stock from the vegetables if needed. Once made, the gravy can be given a fast boil just before serving so that it is piping hot.

Roast Potatoes

Roasting potatoes in goose fat gives them a wonderful flavour, as does cooking them in beef dripping when roasting beef.

Peel the potatoes and cut into even-sized pieces. Place in a saucepan, add a pinch of salt and pour on enough water to come 2.5cm/1" up the side of the pan. Cover. Stand the pan on the boiling plate and bring to the boil. Boil for 3-4 minutes. Drain. Return the potatoes to the dry pan, put on the lid and shake the pan well to fluff the outside of the potatoes (this is only necessary with floury varieties). Add sufficient fat to the saucepan to coat the potatoes. Line a baking tray with Bake-O-Glide and tip in the potatoes. Spread them out evenly.
Hang the tin on the second set of runners from the top of the roasting oven and roast for 30 minutes (with some Agas you may need to turn the tray round after 20 minutes for even-browning). Move the tray to the floor of the oven for 20 minutes to crisp the bottom of the potatoes. Space may mean that you start on the floor and move the potatoes to the top when the meat is out. Serve immediately.

If the roast potatoes are cooked before you are ready for them, remove from the oven and put to one side. Return to the roasting oven to heat through for 10-15 minutes before serving. Don't be tempted to put them in the simmering oven, as they will loose their crispness.

Brussels Sprouts with Chestnuts

Brussels sprouts should be cooked quickly to keep their sweet flavour, colour and crispness, while the addition of chestnuts adds a wonderful richness to the dish.

450g/1lb Brussels sprouts
200g/7oz cooked chestnuts
25g/1oz butter

Trim the sprouts, removing any yellowing leaves. Do not cut a cross in the stalk end. Pour enough water into a saucepan to come 2.5cm/1" up the side of the pan. Add a pinch of salt, cover with a lid and bring to the boil.

Add the sprouts, return to the boil and boil rapidly until the sprouts are just cooked when tested with a sharp knife. Drain well and return to the saucepan. Add the chestnuts and the butter, re-cover and leave to stand for 1-2 minutes, until the butter has melted and the chestnuts are warm. Serve immediately.

Roast Pheasant

Hen pheasant is the best for roasting and ideally it should have been hung for about 7-10 days. Ask your butcher or game dealer if in doubt. A young bird is best for roasting, so ask when buying. A brace of pheasant – a hen and a cock served together, will serve 6 people. If you stuff the birds, remember to increase the cooking time a little.

1 hen pheasant
50g/2oz butter
225g/8oz large white grapes
4 tablespoons brandy
150ml/$\frac{1}{4}$ pint chicken or pheasant stock
1 teaspoon cornflour
Salt and pepper

Spread the pheasant with 25g/1oz of the butter. Place in a roasting tin and hang on the third set of runners from the top of the roasting oven. Roast for 45 minutes. Meanwhile, whiz half the grapes in a blender and then sieve. Halve and de-seed the remaining grapes. When the pheasant is cooked lift it onto a warm serving plate and allow to rest.

Pour the brandy into the roasting pan and stand on the simmering plate. Heat the brandy and then ignite it. When the flame has died down, pour in the stock and the grape juice and scrape in any bits from the bottom of the pan. Blend the cornflour with a little water and pour into the sauce. Bubble and allow the sauce to thicken. Season and stir in the halved grapes and the remaining butter. Carve the pheasant and serve with some grape sauce.

Serves 4

Roast Beef

For the best beef find a good butcher who can supply well butchered and hung beef from a reliable source. I prefer beef sirloin, boned and rolled with some fat on the joint for flavour and succulence. Topside is also popular with less fat than sirloin, but I would only consider this from a good butcher as it can become very dry during roasting. Whatever type of beef you choose it should be roasted in the roasting oven where there should be ample space to also start the roast vegetables.

Weigh the joint and place in a roasting tin. If you would like to season the meat sprinkle on some spices, herbs or just some pepper, but not salt as this can dry out the meat. If the joint has very little fat then smear a little soft butter or vegetable oil over the top. Hang the tin on the third set of runners from the top of the roasting oven and roast for:

Rare
10 minutes per 450g/1lb plus 10 minutes
Medium
15 minutes per 450g/1lb plus 15 minutes
Well done
20 minutes per 450g/1lb plus 20 minutes

If the joint begins to brown too much, move to a lower position and slide a tray of roast vegetables above to prevent further browning. Allow the meat to rest for at least 30 minutes after roasting and before carving.

Yorkshire Puddings

You can cook these puddings before the beef goes in the oven, even the day before, and then reheat. If you try and cook them after the meat, the heat will be too low in the Aga to make them rise and become crisp. The puddings can also be frozen.

Beef dripping or sunflower oil
225g/8oz plain flour
Pinch salt
2 eggs
Approximately 300ml/$\frac{1}{2}$ pint milk

I use a deep muffin tin to make individual puddings. The heat from the deep sides of the tin helps to make them rise. Put a little dripping or half a teaspoon of oil into each muffin tin. Place the tray on the floor of the roasting oven.

Meanwhile, make the batter by placing the flour and the salt in a mixing bowl. Add the eggs and a few tablespoons of milk. Using a balloon whisk, gradually whisk the flour and eggs together, adding more milk to make a smooth batter, the consistency of thick double cream.

By the time the batter is ready, the pan will be very hot and the fat smoking. Pour batter into the tins using either a jug or a ladle. Hang the shelf on the third set of runners from the top of the roasting oven, slide in the muffin tray and cook the puddings for 35-40 minutes, until risen and golden. If your oven tends to cook more on one side, you may have to turn the tray round half way through cooking – don't worry the puddings will not collapse! To warm before serving, return the puddings to the roasting oven for 8-10 minutes.

Makes 12 individual Yorkshire puddings

Roast Haunch of Venison

Haunch of venison, or the prime leg cut, is tender with very little fat and a delicate flavour. Some people like to marinade the joint but I prefer to lard it a little with pork fat. You will need to equip yourself with a larding needle from a good kitchen shop, unless you can persuade your butcher to do the job for you!

2-2.5kg/4$\frac{1}{2}$-5lb haunch of venison
Pork back fat, cut into strips 5mm/$\frac{1}{4}$"
   wide
50g/2oz butter, softened

Lard the joint with strips of pork fat. Thread the fat through the eye of the larding needle and thread a strip of fat through the meat. The joint will look spiked with white strips. If you can't find a larding needle, cut slits in the haunch and plug then with a piece of pork fat, pushed in with the handle of a teaspoon.

Place the prepared joint in a roasting tin and smear well with butter. Hang the roasting tin on the second set of runners from the bottom of the roasting oven and baste the venison every 15 minutes or so.

Roast for
15 minutes per 450g/1lb for a large joint
20 minutes per 450g/1lb for a small joint,
   less than 1.6kg/4lb

Remove the joint from the oven and leave to rest for 20 minutes before carving. The meat will be pink, but will carry on 'cooking' even after carving and should be tender and succulent when eaten.

To carve a haunch of venison, cut slices parallel to the bone.

Serves 6-8

Roast Goose

A good quality flavoursome free-range goose is not always readily available, so be sure to order in plenty of time for Christmas. A bird weighing a 5.5kg/12lb is just enough to just feed 8 people. Put the rack on its lowest position in the roasting tin. Stuff the goose and weigh. Prick the skin all over and rub with salt. Place the goose on the rack. Hang the tin on the third set of runners from the top of the roasting oven and roast for 15 minutes per 450g/1lb plus 15 minutes. During the roasting time you will probably have to pour the fat from the roasting tin. Save the fat for roasting potatoes (see page 50). As goose is fatty there is no need to baste the bird during roasting. Remove from the oven and leave to rest for 20-30 minutes before carving.

Christmas Nut Loaf

This is a terrific recipe for the much-maligned nut loaf – I have cooked it many times at Christmas for both vegetarians and nut-lovers to great acclaim. Even meat-eaters love it!

1 tablespoon olive oil
1 medium onion, peeled and finely
    chopped
225g/8oz chestnuts
50g/2oz brazil nuts
110g/4oz fresh wholemeal breadcrumbs
1 tablespoon chopped fresh parsley
Salt and pepper
150ml/$\frac{1}{4}$ pint vegetable stock
110g/4oz blue Stilton

Heat the oil in a frying pan and cook the onion until soft but not brown. Chop the nuts. I use a food processor for this to get a mixture of very finely chopped and some chunky nuts. Stir in the breadcrumbs, parsley and a seasoning of salt and pepper. Mix in the cooked onion and the stock.

Grease and line a $\frac{1}{2}$kg/1lb loaf tin. Spoon half the nut mixture into the base of the tin and smooth off. Crumble over the Stilton and top with the remaining nut mixture. Smooth the top and cover loosely with foil.

Put the shelf on the bottom set of runners of the roasting oven and put in the nut loaf. Bake for 30 minutes. Remove the loaf and allow it to rest for 5 minutes before turning out onto a serving plate. Serve warm.

Serves 4

Apple-glazed Parsnip Purée

I love this recipe – it offers a slightly different way to serve parsnips, and is a winning combination with pork, ham or sausages. Provided that the apple slices on the top are brushed with lemon juice to prevent browning, this dish can be prepared in advance – even a whole day before it is to be eaten – and then finally baked just before serving.

1kg/2¼lb parsnips, peeled and roughly chopped
Salt and pepper
2 large cooking apples, peeled, cored and thinly sliced
Juice ½ lemon
1 teaspoon sugar

Put the prepared parsnips in a saucepan and add enough water to come 2.5cm/1" up the sides of the pan. Cover and bring the water to the boil. Boil for 1 minute and then drain all the water from the pan. Re-cover and put the parsnips in the simmering oven for 35-40 minutes, or until the parsnips are soft enough to mash. Drain the parsnips and mash well.

Butter a shallow oven-proof dish and spread in half the parsnip purée. Cover the parsnip layer with half the apple slices then spoon over the remaining parsnip. Neatly arrange the remaining apple slices over the top. Brush the apples with lemon juice and sprinkle over the sugar.

Hang the shelf on the third set of runners from the top of the roasting oven. Bake for about 25-30 minutes, until the apple is cooked and starting to brown. Serve immediately.

Serves 4-6

Roast Winter Roots

All root vegetables can be roasted, not just potatoes and parsnips. Use any combination that you like. I think this is one of the best ways of cooking vegetables in the Aga, the roasting really bringing out the flavour of the vegetables.

1.5kg/3lb 5oz mixed root vegetables such as, Parsnip, celeriac, turnip, beetroot, sweet potato
4 tablespoons olive oil
1 tablespoon of lemon juice (if using uncooked beetroot)
12 shallots, peeled
Salt and pepper

Peel the vegetables in the usual way and cut them into even-sized chunks. Set the beetroot aside. Bring a roomy pan of water to the boil and plunge in the vegetables, cover and parboil for 3-4 minutes. Drain well. Return them to the dry pan and shake, with the lid on, to roughen their edges slightly. Pour over the oil and toss the vegetables well. Tip onto a baking tray lined with Bake-O-Glide.

If you are cooking the beetroot, first toss it in the lemon juice, this prevents the colour leaching into the other vegetables. Add the beetroot to the vegetable selection on the tray. Toss the shallots in a little oil and add to the tray. Add a little salt and pepper. Hang the tin on the second set of runners from the top of the roasting oven and roast for 30 minutes, then put the tin on the floor of the oven for 10-15 minutes to finish the roasting. This saves having to turn the vegetables over.

Serves 6

Lime-glazed Winter Vegetables

This glazing gives root vegetables a gloriously sticky finish.

A selection of root vegetables, such as, potatoes, celeriac, parsnip, swede, sweet potato – enough to cover the base of the small baking tray
2 tablespoons sunflower oil
Grated zest and juice 3 limes
1 tablespoon soft brown sugar
1 teaspoon ground coriander

Peel the vegetables and cut into large dice. Place in a saucepan and pour in enough water to come 2.5cm/1" up the sides of the pan. Add a little salt. Cover. Bring to the boil. Boil for 1-2 minutes and then drain off the water. Re-cover and place the pan in the simmering oven for 15 minutes. Tip the vegetables into a colander, drain well and then pat dry with kitchen paper. Place the remaining ingredients in a basin and add the vegetables. Toss well to coat in the glaze. Season and toss again. Tip onto a small baking tray lined with Bake-O-Glide. Hang the tray on the third set of runners from the top of the roasting oven and cook until brown and sticky, about 20-25 minutes.

Serves 8

Braised Red Cabbage with Raspberry Vinegar

I think this is a luscious way to cook red cabbage. Although raspberry vinegar is quite expensive to buy, it is well worth it for this wonderful dish. Serve the cabbage with ham or pork.

25g/1oz butter
1 small red cabbage, shredded fairly finely
1 onion, peeled and thinly sliced
50g/2oz dried apricots, chopped
1 teaspoon allspice
6 cloves
50g/2oz soft brown sugar
150ml/$\frac{1}{4}$ pint raspberry vinegar
Salt and pepper

Melt the butter in a flameproof casserole. Add the cabbage and onion. Stir to coat in the butter. Cover and cook gently for 5 minutes. Add all the remaining ingredients and season with salt and pepper.

Cover and gently bring to the boil. When bubbling, move to the simmering oven and cook for 1-1$\frac{1}{2}$ hours, or until the cabbage is tender.

Serves 8

Boxing Day

Boxing Day for some people means just relaxing and eating leftovers. I like to watch a Mummers play or go for a good long country walk, but for others it's another day of entertaining and cooking meals for family and friends.

A richly flavoured casserole with a dish of simply baked potatoes may be just what is needed on a cold winter's day. For this reason I have included some classic winter favourites such as Venison Casserole with Pickled Walnuts (page 74) and Guinea Fowl with Prunes and Apples (page 77).

Some of these recipes in this section can of course be cooked in advance and heated through on the day, enabling you to enjoy a well-earned rest. There are many other delicious recipes in the Lunches, Dinners and Suppers section (page 86) that you may also find appropriate for Boxing Day.

Pheasant Breasts with Orange and Walnut

Pheasant breasts are available from most supermarkets now, or if you are lucky enough to have a lot of pheasant to hand, you can use just the breast meat for this recipe and make a wonderful stock with the rest of the bird.

4 pheasant breasts, from 2 birds
2 tablespoons seasoned flour
2 oranges
50g/2oz walnut pieces
1 tablespoon walnut oil
150ml/$\frac{1}{4}$ pint stock
15g/$\frac{1}{2}$oz cold butter
Salt and pepper

Put the seasoned flour onto a plate and grate the rind of one orange into the flour. Coat the pheasant breasts with the flour. Squeeze the juice from the rindless orange and reserve. Peel and segment the remaining orange. Set aside. Stand a sauté pan on the simmering plate and add the walnuts. Shake in the pan for a minute and then set aside. Heat the walnut oil in the pan and when hot add the floured pheasant breasts, skin side down. Move the pan to the floor of the roasting oven and cook for about 6 minutes. Remove the pheasant from the pan and keep warm.

Add the stock and the reserved orange juice to the pan, scraping up any bits and then return the pheasant breasts to the pan, skin side uppermost. Allow the juices to bubble and return the pan to the floor of the roasting oven for a further 5-8 minutes, until cooked. Remove the pheasant breasts from the pan and keep warm. Strain the pan juices into a clean saucepan and bring to the boil. Reduce the sauce until it has become syrupy. Whisk in the cold butter.

Cut the pheasant breasts into slices and serve with the orange segments, walnuts and a little sauce.

Serves 4

Herb-Stuffed Leg of Lamb

The herb stuffing adds freshness and can be made in advance and kept in the freezer. Ask your butcher to tunnel bone the leg of lamb, which will make stuffing the joint easier – keep the bones and roast with the meat to add flavour to the gravy.

1 leg of lamb, about 2kg/4$\frac{1}{2}$lb, tunnel-boned
16 cloves garlic, peeled
Salt and pepper
Olive oil

For the Provencal breadcrumbs
100g/3$\frac{1}{2}$oz fresh breadcrumbs
Small bunch of fresh parsley, stalks removed
4 sprigs rosemary or thyme, leaves picked from the stalks
2 cloves garlic, peeled and chopped
2 tablespoons olive oil
Salt and pepper

Spread the breadcrumbs on a baking tray and put in the simmering oven to dry for 4-6 hours. Put the herbs and garlic in a blender, whiz and then add the dried breadcrumbs and the olive oil. Season and then whizz again.

Bring a small saucepan of water to boil and put in the peeled cloves of garlic. Blanch for a minute or two and drain. Repeat. This blanching will soften the garlic and help to remove any harsh flavours. Slice the garlic into the breadcrumbs and add 2-3 tablespoons of olive oil. Season with salt and pepper. Mix well. Pack the stuffing into the boned lamb, mould the leg and re-tie if necessary. Rub the joint with a little oil and if there is any stuffing left, you can rub this over the lamb too. If you have the chopped bones, put them in the base of the small roasting tin. Sit the lamb on top of the bones.

Hang the tin on the third set of runners from the top of the roasting oven for 30 minutes. Pour in 300ml/$\frac{1}{2}$ pint water and move the tin to the bottom set of runners. Roast for 1 hour. Remove the lamb from the oven, put on a serving plate to keep warm while resting. Remove and discard the bones from the tin. Pour 300ml/$\frac{1}{2}$ pint water into the roasting tin and stand on the simmering plate. Bring the liquid to the boil, scraping in any caramelised bits from the bottom of the tin. Serve the carved lamb with the pan juices.

Serves 8

Venison Casserole with Pickled Walnuts

A rich, winter casserole that can be made in advance and frozen – add the pickled walnuts after re-heating.

700g/1$\frac{1}{2}$lb diced venison
150ml/5fl oz red wine vinegar
2 bay leaves
Seasoned flour
25g/1oz butter
1 tablespoon olive oil
2 red onions, peeled, halved and finely sliced
8 juniper berries, lightly crushed
110g/4oz chestnut mushrooms, wiped and sliced
150ml/$\frac{1}{4}$ pint vegetable or beef stock
150ml/$\frac{1}{4}$ pint red wine
2 tablespoons redcurrant jelly
Salt and pepper
12 pickled walnuts

Place the trimmed venison in a non-metallic bowl. Pour over the wine vinegar and add the bay leaves and a seasoning of pepper. Cover and leave somewhere cool, to marinate overnight.

Drain the venison, reserving the liquid. Dry the meat and toss in seasoned flour. Melt the butter in a flameproof casserole and sauté the onions and juniper berries until the onion is just softening. Add the mushrooms, fry for 2-3 minutes and then add the meat. Stir the meat into the onion mixture and then add the reserved marinade, the stock, wine and redcurrant jelly. Season with salt and pepper, cover and bring the casserole to the boil.

Once the casserole is boiling, leave it to bubble for 2-3 minutes and then move it to the simmering oven for 2- 2 $\frac{1}{2}$ hours, until the meat is tender. Stir in the drained pickled walnuts, heat through and adjust the seasoning. Serve hot with creamy mashed potatoes.

Serves 6

Venison, Beef and Cranberry Pie

This is really a cheat's pie! The meat is casseroled on its own and then served with squares of pastry as a garnish. If you are a pastry fan then you might like to double the quantity of pastry. You will find that the chestnuts are easier to peel if you soak them first in hot water. Vacuum-packed chestnuts also work well in this dish. As with many slowly cooked meat dishes, I think this has the best flavour if it is cooked one day and then chilled and re-heated for serving the next. Cook the pastry just before serving for best results.

700g/1½lb stewing venison, cubed
300g/10½oz braising steak, cubed
1 level teaspoon black peppercorns, crushed
6 juniper berries, crushed
3 bay leaves
1 teaspoon chopped thyme
150ml/¼ pint Marsala
2 cloves garlic, peeled and crushed
4 tablespoons olive oil
200g/7oz streaky bacon, rind removed and chopped
1 tablespoon tomato purée
2 tablespoons flour
300ml/½ pint beef stock
225g/8oz shallots, peeled
225g/8oz chestnuts, cooked
110g/4oz cranberries
Juice and strip of zest from 1 orange
375g pack ready-rolled puff pastry
1 egg, beaten to glaze the pastry

Put the venison, beef, peppercorns, juniper berries, bay leaves, thyme, Marsala, garlic and olive oil in a large non-metallic bowl. Mix well. Cover and leave somewhere cool, to marinate overnight.

Put the bacon in a flameproof casserole and heat gently until the fat runs. Cook until crisp. Drain the meat and reserve the marinade, add the meat to the pan and sprinkle over the flour. Stir well. Add the tomato purée to the stock and pour over the meat followed by the reserved marinade. Add the shallots, chestnuts and cranberries. Remove a long strip of peel from the orange and bury this in the meat. Squeeze the juice from the orange and pour over the meat. Season. Cover and slowly bring to the boil. Bubble for 2-3 minutes and then move the casserole to the simmering oven for 2-3 hours, or until the meat is tender.

About 20 minutes before serving, unroll the pastry and lay it on a large baking tray. Cut the pastry into six even portions. Mark the top of each piece of pastry with the back of a knife to decorate. Brush the pastry with beaten egg to glaze.

Hang the tin on the third set of runners from the top of the roasting oven for 15 minutes, until risen and golden brown. Divide the meat between six warm plates, spoon over the sauce and top with a pastry shape.

Serves 6

Guinea Fowl with Prunes and Apples

The inclusion of guinea fowl and harissa gives this casserole just a little unexpected edge. It's a shame that more people don't hunt out this delicious bird as they are missing out on a very delicately flavoured meat with just a hint of gaminess.

1 large onion, peeled and chopped
1 large carrot, peeled and chopped
2 sticks celery, trimmed and sliced
8 joints of guinea fowl
500ml/1 pint red wine
1 tablespoon chopped thyme
2 bay leaves
175g/6oz ready-to-eat prunes
2 tablespoons vegetable oil
3 cloves garlic, peeled and crushed
1 teaspoon harissa paste
1 tablespoon tomato purée
1 tablespoon flour
225g/8oz streaky bacon, rind removed and
    each rasher cut into 4
2 eating apples, cored and sliced

Put the onion, carrot, celery and guinea fowl in a non-metallic bowl. Pour over 400ml/^{3}/4 pint wine. Add the thyme and bay leaves and a seasoning of salt and pepper. Cover and leave somewhere cool to marinate overnight.

Put the prunes in a basin and pour over the remaining100ml/^{1}/4 pint of wine. Leave to stand.

Drain the meat and vegetables and reserve the marinade. Heat the oil in a flameproof casserole. If you like a very brown tinge to the meat then brown the guinea fowl in the oil and set aside. Cook the drained vegetables for 4-5 minutes and then stir in the Harissa paste, tomato purée and then sprinkle over the flour. Stir well and cook for 1 minute before gradually adding the marinade. Bring to

the boil and then add the meat. Cover and boil for 2-3 minutes. Move the casserole to the simmering oven and cook for 1 hour.

Place the bacon pieces in a frying pan and place the pan on the floor of the roasting oven. Cook until the fat is beginning to run and the bacon is crisping. Add the apple slices and cook until golden.

Remove the casserole from the oven and take out the guinea fowl, keep warm. Strain the sauce through a sieve. Return the meat to the rinsed out pan and add the strained sauce, the prunes and their marinade. Heat through.

Serve each portion with some apple and bacon.

Serves 8

Mashed Potatoes Bolognese Style

450g/1 lb potatoes, peeled
45g/1½oz butter, melted
100ml/4fl oz milk
6 tablespoons finely grated Parmesan
  cheese
Freshly grated nutmeg

Chop the potatoes into even-sized pieces and place in a saucepan with 2.5cm/1" water. Cover with a lid and bring to the boil. Boil for 1 minute and then drain off the water. Put in the simmering oven and cook until soft enough to mash. Drain well. Mash the potatoes with the melted butter. Heat the milk until just below boiling point and beat into the potatoes 2-3 tablespoons at a time. Half way through add most of the milk, beat in the grated cheese and then add some of the remaining milk, though not enough to make the potatoes runny. Add seasoning and serve immediately.

Serves 6

Potato and Horseradish Gratin

1kg/1¼lb potatoes, peeled and very thinly
  sliced
300 ml/½ pint double cream
150ml/¼ pint crème fraîche
300ml/½ pint full fat milk
6 tablespoons creamed horseradish

Butter a shallow ovenproof dish and layer the potatoes, seasoning each layer with salt and pepper. Pour the cream, crème fraîche and the milk into a saucepan and stand on the simmering plate until almost boiling. Stir in the horseradish sauce and pour the liquid slowly over the potatoes. Put the shelf on the floor of the roasting oven and slide in the dish of potatoes. Bake the gratin for 40 minutes and check to see if the potatoes are cooked through. If the potatoes are still firm or the sauce is too runny either cover the dish with foil, or for a 3 or 4-oven Aga move the dish to the bottom set of runners of the baking oven. Cook for a further 20 minutes until the potatoes are soft.

Serves 6

" Boxing Day for some people means just relaxing and eating leftovers.

But for others it's another day of entertaining and cooking meals for family and friends."

Spicy Red Cabbage

75g/3oz butter
2 red onions, peeled and finely chopped
1 medium red cabbage, finely sliced
Juice 1 lemon
2 tablespoons red wine vinegar
2 teaspoons soft brown sugar
1 cinnamon stick
4 cloves
1 star anise
Salt and pepper

Melt the butter in a roomy flameproof casserole or saucepan. Add the onions and cook gently until soft but not browning. Stir in the cabbage, sugar, lemon juice, vinegar, sugar, cinnamon, cloves and star anise. Coat all the ingredients with the butter and season with salt and pepper. Cover and heat for 2-3 minutes on the simmering plate and then move to the simmering oven for about an hour, or until the cabbage is cooked.

Serves 8

Butter-Roasted Cabbage

75g/3oz butter
1 shallot, peeled and sliced
2 bay leaves
1 large cabbage, cut into quarters
100ml/3$\frac{1}{2}$fl oz stock

Melt the butter in a small saucepan and cook the shallot and the bay leaves until the shallot is soft. Place the cabbage into a casserole or deep baking dish and pour the butter mixture over. Hang the shelf on the bottom set of runners of the roasting oven and put in the cabbage. Roast for 10 minutes and then spoon over the stock, continue to roast the cabbage for a further 10-15 minutes. Spoon the pan juices over the cabbage on serving.

Serves 4

Parmesan and Mustard Parsnips

This is an irresistible variation on the classic dish of roast parsnips.

700g/1$\frac{1}{2}$lb small parsnips, peeled and
   halved lengthways
50g/2oz butter
2 tablespoons olive oil
110g/4oz grated Parmesan cheese
5 teaspoons mustard powder

Place the parsnips in a saucepan and pour on enough water to come 2.5cm/1" up the sides of the pan. Cover and bring to the boil on the boiling plate. Simmer for 2-3 minutes. Drain well. Put the oil and butter in the small roasting tin and place on the floor of the roasting oven to heat.

On a plate, mix together the Parmesan cheese and the mustard powder. Roll the blanched parsnips in the cheese and mustard mixture. Once the parsnips have all been coated, place them carefully in the hot roasting tin and turn them in the hot oil.

Hang the tin on the second set of runners from the top of the roasting oven and roast for 30-40 minutes, or until cooked and golden brown.

Serves 8

Lunches, Dinners and Suppers for the Festive Season

Over the past few years more and more people have been taking a longer break from work over the Christmas period. Whilst it's an excellent opportunity to catch up with old friends and distant family it does tend to mean that a lot more cooking is required.

After all the hard work of Christmas Day most of us would rather not be stuck in the kitchen for any longer than we have to, so here are a few delicious, quickly prepared meals that take a minimum amount of time and effort. You could try dishes such as Chicken and Mango Stir-fry (page 89) and Sugar-glazed Gammon with Butterbean Mash (page 92), as well as some great meals that can made made in advance, such as the outstanding Chicken Liver and Cranberry Terrine (page 88), or the delicious and surprising Mascarpone and Gorgonzola Tart with Balsamic Onions (page 103).

Chicken Liver and Cranberry Terrine with a Cranberry Confit

Make this excellent terrine in advance and serve it cold with salad and good, fresh crusty bread.

For the Confit
450g/1lb cranberries
110g/4oz caster sugar
300ml/½ pint red wine
2 tablespoons red wine vinegar
Finely grated rind and juice 1 orange

Place all the ingredients in a saucepan, stir and cover. Stand on the simmering plate and allow the mixture to come to the boil. Move the pan to the simmering oven and cook for 1 hour. Remove from the oven, tip into a dish and cool.

For the Terrine
225g/8oz streaky bacon, rind removed
500g/1lb 2oz chicken livers
500g/1lb 2oz minced pork
1 large onion, peeled and chopped
2 cloves garlic, peeled and chopped
2 tablespoons brandy
75g/3oz cranberries
4 bay leaves
Salt and pepper

Stretch all but 2 rashers of bacon with a table knife. Use the stretched rashers to line a 1kg / 2lb loaf tin. Dice the remaining rashers of bacon and mix with the chicken livers, minced pork, chopped onion and garlic in a food processor and whiz. Tip into a bowl and season with salt and pepper. Stir in the brandy and the cranberries.

Spoon the mixture into the lined loaf tin. Lay the bay leaves on top. Cover the top with a double layer of foil. Stand the loaf tin in the small roasting tin and pour round enough boiling water to come a third of the way up the sides of the loaf tin.

Hang the roasting tin on the bottom set of runners of the roasting oven and cook for 30 minutes. Move the roasting tin to the simmering oven for a further 2 hours. Remove the loaf tin from the roasting tin and press down the pâté with weights (I use tins from the cupboard) until cold.

Once cold, remove from the tin and serve sliced with the Cranberry Confit.

Serves 8-10

Chicken and Mango Stir-fry

This is such a wonderfully quick and tasty dish. I have specified using a bag of ready-prepared stir-fry vegetables, but you can, of course, make up your own mix from whatever you have in the fridge.

2 mugs basmati rice
Salt
450g/1lb boneless chicken breast, sliced
    into strips
3 tablespoons light vegetable oil
1 bunch spring onions, trimmed and sliced
    diagonally
1 x 2.5cm/1" cube ginger, peeled and
    grated
1 clove garlic, peeled and chopped
1 ripe mango, peeled and the flesh cubed
350g/12oz pack ready-prepared stir-fry
    vegetables
3 tablespoons light soy sauce
1 tablespoon sweet chilli sauce

To cook the rice, measure the rice into a saucepan and add 3 mugs of water. Add a pinch of salt. Cover and bring to the boil. As soon as the water boils, move the pan to the simmering oven. The rice should be cooked in 12 minutes, having absorbed all the water. Cover and return to the simmering oven until the stir-fry is ready.

Put the empty wok on the boiling plate for 10 minutes whilst preparing the ingredients. Toss the chicken strips in 2 tablespoons of oil and then add to the hot wok. Stir-fry for 4-5 minutes until the chicken is lightly golden brown and cooked through. Remove the chicken from the wok and keep warm.

Add the remaining tablespoon of oil to the wok and stir-fry the onions, ginger and garlic. Stir well and then add the mango and the vegetables. Stir well for 2 minutes and then return the chicken to the wok. Pour over the soy sauce and the chilli sauce. Continue to stir and cook for 2 minutes, until the chicken is piping hot and the vegetables softening. Serve immediately with the hot rice.

Serves 4

Citrus Chicken with Red Onions

I think that this has to be one of the quickest chicken dishes to prepare that I know. The oranges and marmalade add a delightful seasonal flavour.

1 orange
1 lemon
4 tablespoons marmalade, preferably
   fine-cut
1 tablespoon olive oil
4 chicken breasts
8 sprigs thyme
2 red onions, peeled
225g/8oz couscous
1 tablespoon olive oil
1 tablespoon chopped fresh parsley

Cut the orange and lemon in half. Squeeze the juice from one half of the orange and one half of the lemon. Pour into a basin and add the marmalade and one tablespoon of olive oil. Season. Mix well.

Slash each chicken breast twice and put a sprig of thyme in each cut. Place in a shallow ovenproof dish. Quarter the onions and put these quarters between the chicken pieces. Cut the lemon and orange halves into 4 chunks each and fit these in between the chicken and onions. Spoon the marmalade mixture over.

Put the shelf on the bottom set of runners of the roasting oven and cook for 25-30 minutes until the chicken is cooked through and golden brown. About 10 minutes before the chicken has cooked, place the couscous in a serving bowl and pour on enough boiling water to come 1cm/$\frac{1}{2}$" above the surface of the couscous. Cover with a lid or plate and stand at the back of the Aga for 10 minutes. Stir the couscous and then stir in the olive oil and chopped parsley.

Slice the chicken pieces, serving one breast per person with some of the roast onion mixture and the couscous. Spoon the juices over.

Serves 4

Sugar-glazed Gammon with Butterbean Mash

I wonder how many of us were put off butterbeans at school. I can honestly say that I suffered from awful school meals and butterbeans were served up weekly to very unappetising effect. This way of serving them has restored my liking for them. You could substitute the butterbeans with other canned beans such as flageolets.

1kg/2¼lb gammon joint, smoked or
    unsmoked, as preferred
600ml/1 pint dry cider
2 tablespoons Demerara sugar
½ teaspoon mustard powder
6 cloves

For the Butterbean Mash
1 tablespoon olive oil
2 cloves garlic, peeled and sliced
1 bunch spring onions, trimmed and sliced
2 x 410g cans butterbeans, drained
4 tablespoons crème fraîche
Salt and pepper

Soak the gammon joint overnight. Place a trivet or old saucer in the base of a saucepan and put in the soaked gammon joint. Pour over the cider (the joint should not be covered in liquid). Cover with a lid and stand on the simmering plate, allowing the liquid to come slowly to the boil. If necessary, pull the pan half off the simmering plate and allow the liquid to gently simmer for 20-30 minutes. Move to the simmering oven for 2 hours.

Remove the ham from the saucepan and cool slightly. Remove the skin and score the fat into diamonds. Place a clove in each diamond. Mix together the mustard and the Demerara sugar. Press this over the scored fat.

Stand the ham on a baking tray lined with Bake-O-Glide. Spoon a little cooking liquid over the lean meat and hang the tin on the third set of runners from the top of the roasting oven for 15-20 minutes, until a golden crust has formed.

Meanwhile prepare the mash. Heat the olive oil in a saucepan and sauté the onions and garlic until soft but not brown. Whiz the butterbeans in a blender or food processor until smooth, or mash with a potato masher. Mix the beans into the onion mixture. Heat through, stirring in the crème fraîche.

If the mixture is still very stiff a little cooking liquid from the meat can be added, but take care not to add too much salt to the beans when adjusting the seasoning.

Serve slices of delicious hot ham with a spoonful of wonderful, faith restoring butterbean mash.

Serves 6

Pork Fillet with Puy Lentils

This is an all-in-one dish for those days that you'd rather not spend huddled in the kitchen cooking for family and friends! The quantity can easily be doubled to feed more people.

4 tablespoons grainy mustard
500g/1lb 2oz pork fillet
1 tablespoon olive oil
400g/14oz Puy lentils
2 medium potatoes, peeled and cut into chunks
2 red onions, peeled and quartered
8 pieces sun-dried tomato
3-4 sprigs thyme
1.2 litres/2 pints vegetable or chicken stock
2 tablespoons chopped fresh parsley
Salt and pepper

Spread 2 tablespoons of mustard over the pork fillet. Heat the oil in a large frying or sauté pan and brown the meat (this can be done on the floor of the roasting oven). Remove the pork from the pan and set aside.

To the pan, add the lentils, potatoes, onions, sun-dried tomatoes, thyme and a seasoning of salt and pepper. Mix the 2 remaining tablespoons of mustard with the stock and pour this over the lentil mixture in the pan. Bring the lentil mixture to the boil, cover and move to the simmering oven for 15 minutes.

Place the pork fillet on top of the lentil mixture and again bring to the boil. Return the pan to the simmering oven for a further 15-20 minutes, or until the pork fillet is cooked. Allow the meat to rest for 5 minutes before slicing. Spoon the lentil mixture onto warm plates and top with slices of pork and a sprinkling of chopped parsley.

Serves 4

The Quickest Salmon en Croute

This is so easy to prepare yet is always impressive. Cooking salmon in pastry keeps the fish moist and the addition of Boursin cheese makes a flavoursome sauce.

2 packets ready-rolled puff pastry
2 long skinless salmon fillets, about
    375g/13oz each
1 large packet Boursin herbed cheese
1 egg, beaten to glaze

Line a large Aga baking tray with a sheet of Bake-O-Glide. Unroll 1 packet of puff pastry onto the baking tray. Lay one salmon fillet down the middle of the pastry. Spread the Boursin cheese over the salmon and then place the second fillet on top. Unroll the second packet of puff pastry and gently lay over the fish, excluding as much air as possible. Press the two pieces of pastry together and trim off any excess, leaving a 2.5cm/1" border. Using the back of a knife, lightly mark a diamond pattern, taking care not to cut through the pastry. Cut a small slit in the middle for steam to escape. Brush well with beaten egg to glaze the pastry.

Hang the tray on the third set of runners from the top of the roasting oven and bake for 20 minutes. The pastry should be risen and golden. Move the tray to the floor of the roasting oven for 5 minutes to crisp the pastry base. Remove from the oven, allow to rest for 5 minutes, then lift onto a serving platter and serve hot.

Serves 8-10

Tagliatelli in a Lemony Sauce

On those days when comfort food such as pasta is needed but the usual tomato sauce doesn't seem to fit the bill, try this quick to prepare lemony pasta. If you happen to have been making a lot of meringues (and over the Christmas period this is quite likely) then this is a good way to use up those spare egg yolks.

3 egg yolks
200ml/7fl oz crème fraîche
Salt and pepper
grated rind and juice of 1 lemon
250g/9oz tagliatelli
200g/7oz frozen petit pois
25g/1oz butter
2 tablespoons chopped fresh parsley
110g/4oz Parmesan, grated
Parmesan shavings to serve

Beat together the egg yolks and 4 tablespoons of the crème fraîche. Season with salt and pepper and set aside. Place the remaining crème fraîche in a saucepan with the lemon rind and heat through gently. Cook gently for 5 minutes and then put at the back of the Aga to allow the flavours to infuse. Bring a large pan of water to the boil and cook the pasta following the packet instructions. Add the petit pois 2-3 minutes before the end of the cooking time. Drain.

Return the drained pasta to the saucepan and stir in the beaten egg yolk mixture, the butter, parsley, lemon juice and the warm crème fraîche. Mix in the grated Parmesan and serve immediately with shavings of Parmesan on top.

Serves 6

Smoked Salmon and Goats' Cheese Roulade

Roulades are much loved, always impress, and are so easy to make. The roulade mixture is especially pliable when baked in an Aga. I have made this dish in a variety of sizes – as a canapé, a starter, and as a main course. Just roll the roulade into the size you need. Try to give the finished roulade time to rest and set, as you will find that it will then be easier to slice. The roulade will freeze for up to one month.

300ml/½ pint milk
50g/2oz butter
50g/2oz flour
Salt and pepper
110g/4oz soft goats' cheese
50g/2oz Parmesan cheese, grated
4 eggs, separated

For the filling
110g/4oz cream cheese
1 tablespoon chopped dill
110g/4oz smoked salmon slices

Line a large Aga baking tray or roasting tin with Bake-O-Glide. Put the milk, butter, flour and a seasoning of salt and pepper in a saucepan. Stand on the simmering plate and whisk until a smooth and glossy sauce has been made. Remove from the heat and stir in the goats' cheese and half the Parmesan cheese. Beat in the egg yolks.

Whisk the egg whites until white and fluffy. Beat 1 tablespoon of egg white into the sauce and then fold in the remaining egg white. Fold the mixture together carefully until the mixture resembles scrambled egg. Spoon the mixture into the lined tin and level off gently.

Hang the tin on the bottom set of runners of the roasting oven and bake for 15-20 minutes, until golden and just firm to the touch. Remove the roulade from the oven and scatter over the remaining Parmesan cheese. Set aside to cool.

Put the cream cheese in a basin and beat in the chopped dill. Turn the roulade out onto a plain sheet of Bake-O-Glide and remove the lining sheet. Spread the roulade with the cream cheese mixture and lay over the slices of smoked salmon. Roll the roulade from the short end, if it is for a main course, or the long end, for a starter, rolling up as tightly as possible. Roll onto a serving plate and allow it to set before slicing.

If freezing, roll the roulade onto a sheet of foil on a baking tray. Open freeze and then wrap when firm. To thaw, unwrap, put on a serving tray and thaw somewhere cool overnight.

Stuffed Peppers with Brie

Theses stuffed peppers can be served as a simple starter, lunch dish or vegetarian dish. The roasting of the peppers brings out their delicious sweetness. If you are serving this for a vegetarian then be sure to choose a tapenade that does not contain anchovies.

4 red peppers
8 teaspoons of olive tapenade
  (about $\frac{1}{2}$ a jar)
8 cherry tomatoes
8 black olives, pitted and chopped
2-3 basil leaves
225g/8 oz Brie
2 tablespoons olive oil

Halve the peppers through the stalks and remove the seeds. Place cut-side uppermost, in a shallow oven-proof dish. Spread the inside of each half of pepper with a teaspoonful of the tapenade. Cut the tomatoes in half and put two halves in each pepper. Divide the olives between the peppers. Tear the basil leaves and scatter onto the peppers. Slice the Brie into 8 slices and place a slice in each pepper half. Drizzle the oil over the peppers.

Hang the shelf on the second set of runners from the bottom of the roasting oven and put in the peppers. Roast for 25-30 minutes until the peppers are tender and the cheese is melting.

Serves 8 as a starter

Wild Mushroom Risotto

Dried porcini mushrooms soaked for half an hour can be used if you can't find fresh ones. The soaking liquid can then be used for cooking the risotto. Crisply cooked bacon can be added at the end if desired.

100g/4oz assorted wild mushrooms,
    sliced
1 medium onion, chopped
2 tablespoons olive oil
50g/2oz butter
1 clove garlic, finely chopped
600-900ml / 1-1$\frac{1}{2}$ pints stock, hot
275g/10oz risotto rice
8 tablespoons white wine
50g/2oz Parmesan, finely grated

Sauté the onion in the oil and half the butter in a deep frying pan on the simmering plate until soft and pale golden. Stir in the garlic and mushrooms.

Stir in the rice until well coated with the butter, add the wine and boil for about 2 minutes until it is absorbed. Gradually add the stock, stirring gently until it is all absorbed and the rice is cooked, about 10-15 minutes. The rice should not become soggy and should have a little sauce around it; you may need all the stock.

Remove from the heat, stir in the butter and most of the cheese. Season to taste and serve with the remaining grated cheese.

Serves 4

Beetroot and Red Wine Risotto

The finished colour of this wonderful dish is quite startling. The beetroot gives the risotto an unusual earthy flavour and is an excellent way of using this under-rated vegetable.

2 tablespoons olive oil
1 red onion, peeled and finely chopped
500g/1lb 2oz Arborio rice
2 raw beetroot, peeled and diced
225ml/8fl oz red wine
1 litre/$1^3/4$ pints hot vegetable stock
Grated rind and juice $^1/_2$ lemon
Parmesan shavings, to serve

Heat the olive oil in a large sauté pan and add the onion. Cook gently until the onion is soft but not brown. Stir in the rice and the beetroot and stir to coat with the oil. Pour over the wine and stir until the wine has been completely absorbed by the rice. Gradually add the stock, a ladle full at a time. Continue to stir, adding more stock until the texture is creamy and the rice al dente. Remove from the heat and stir in the lemon rind and juice and adjust the seasoning. Serve topped with shavings of Parmesan cheese.

Serves 4 as a main course or 6 as a starter

Mascarpone and Gorgonzola Tart with Balsamic Onions

Though very rich, this delicious tart is surprisingly light to eat. The onions can be made in advance and stored in the fridge – I usually double the quantity, as these balsamic onions are also good with cold meats and cheeses. For an even better flavour make them at least a day before eating.

1 pack chilled shortcrust pastry or
   175g/6oz shortcrust pastry
4 eggs
500g/1lb Mascarpone
225g/8oz Gorgonzola
Pepper

Roll out the pastry to line a 23cm/9" shallow flan tin. Chill. Put the eggs, Mascarpone, Gorgonzola and a grinding of pepper in a blender and whiz until smooth. Pour into the pastry case.

Put the tart on the floor of the roasting oven and slide the cold shelf onto the second set of runners from the bottom. Bake for 20-25 minutes until set and golden brown.

For the Balsamic Onions
3 tablespoons olive oil
450g/1lb red onion, peeled and finely
   sliced
2 tablespoons soft brown sugar
2 tablespoons balsamic vinegar

Heat the oil in a saucepan and add the onions. Stir well and cover with a lid. Heat for 1 minute on the simmering plate and then move the pan to the simmering oven for 1 hour. The onions should then be very soft. Remove the lid and stand the pan on the simmering plate, add the sugar and bubble to caramelise the onions. Stir in the vinegar and cook on the floor of the roasting oven for 5-10 minutes, until thick. Cool and then store in a jar in the fridge.

Serves 6-8

Hot Feta Cheese

This simple starter has a delightfully fresh flavour and so is particularly suitable as a counter balance to the many rich dishes that are traditionally eaten during the Christmas holiday period.

2 x 250g blocks feta cheese
2 tablespoons olive oil
2 red chillies, seeded and finely sliced
2 teaspoons finely chopped thyme
4 tomatoes, finely sliced

Cut the blocks of feta in half and then cut through the depth of each block to make 8 slices. Lay these slices on a baking tray lined with Bake-O-Glide. Drizzle over the olive oil and scatter over the chopped chilli and thyme. Lay a tomato slice on the top of each piece of cheese.

About 5 minutes before serving the cheese, hang the tray on the top set of runners of the roasting oven. Cook until the tomatoes are softening and the feta is sizzling around the edges. Serve with bread.

Serves 8

Roast Beetroot with Goats' Cheese

Roasting beetroot, as in this starter, brings out all its lovely sweet flavour.

2 large beetroot, peeled and cut into
  even-sized wedges
2 tablespoons olive oil
Salt and pepper
1 bag rocket
200g/7oz firm goats' cheese, cut into
  chunks
110g/4oz semi-dried tomatoes

For the dressing
100ml/3$\frac{1}{2}$fl oz olive oil
2 tablespoons balsamic vinegar

Toss the prepared beetroot in the olive oil and season with salt and pepper. Lay it out on a baking tray lined with Bake-O-Glide. Hang the tin on the third set of runners from the top of the roasting oven and roast the beetroot for 40 minutes, or until cooked through. Cool.

Lay the rocket on six serving plates and scatter over the beetroot, then the goats' cheese and the tomato halves.
Mix together the oil and vinegar for the dressing and drizzle over the beetroot.

Serves 6 as a starter

Leek and Stilton Soup

A classic leek and potato soup finished with some seasonal Stilton. This makes a wonderful lunch or supper dish served simply with freshly baked bread.

50g/2oz butter
350g/12oz leeks, washed, trimmed and
  sliced
2 medium potatoes, peeled and cut into
  chunks
2 bay leaves
250g/9oz blue Stilton
4 tablespoons plain yoghurt
Salt and pepper

Melt the butter in a large saucepan and add the leeks. Toss in the butter and then sauté, with a lid on, until softening but not browning. Add the potatoes and the bay leaves and toss in the butter. Pour in 1 litre/1 $^{3}/_{4}$ pints of water. Cover and bring to the boil. Once boiling, move the pan to the simmering oven and cook for 30-40 minutes, or until the potatoes are cooked.

Remove the bay leaves and crumble in half of the Stilton. Purée the soup in a blender. Season with pepper and a little salt, not too much because the Stilton adds some salt to the soup. Stir in the yoghurt and serve with the remaining Stilton crumbled on top.

This soup can be frozen for up to 1 month.

Serves 4-6

Cream of Celeriac and Garlic Soup

Don't be put off by the amount of garlic, it adds to the richness of the soup.

3 bulbs garlic
2 tablespoons olive oil
1 onion, peeled and chipped
2 whole celeriac, peeled and roughly
   diced
1.2 litres/2 pints vegetable or turkey stock
284ml/$\frac{1}{2}$ pint double cream
Salt and pepper

Break the bulbs of garlic onto a baking tray. Hang the tray from the third set of runners from the top of the roasting oven and roast for 15-20 minutes, until soft and beginning to brown. Set aside to cool.

Heat the olive oil in a large saucepan and sauté the onion until soft but not brown. Add the celeriac, toss in the oil and cook slowly on the simmering plate while dealing with the garlic. Squeeze the cloves of garlic from their skins into the pan. Discard the skins. Add the stock, cover the pan and bring to the boil. Move to the simmering oven and cook for 40-45 minutes, until the celeriac is soft.

Blend the soup until smooth. Return to the rinsed out pan and stir in the cream. Heat gently and adjust the seasoning.

This soup can be frozen for up to 1 month.

Serves 6-8

Corn and Ginger Soup

Sometimes over the Christmas holiday I crave fresh-flavoured light food. This soup fits the bill perfectly. It is also very easy to make from store-cupboard ingredients.

1 tablespoon vegetable oil
4 spring onions, trimmed and finely
  chopped
1 tablespoon finely chopped fresh ginger
1 x 300g can corn nibblets, drained
1 litre/1¾ pints chicken or vegetable
  stock
1 tablespoon rice wine or dry sherry
Salt and pepper
1 teaspoon sugar
2 tablespoons light soy sauce

For the garnish
1 spring onion, sliced
1 teaspoon sesame oil

Heat the oil in a large saucepan and add the onions and ginger. Stir for a minute and then add the corn. Pour in the stock, the rice wine, a seasoning of salt and pepper, sugar and the soy sauce. Cover the pan and bring to the boil. Once boiling, move the pan to the simmering oven for 10-15 minutes.

To serve, ladle the soup into warm bowls and garnish with the sliced spring onion and a little sesame oil.

Serves 6-8

Almond and Broccoli Stir-fry

I love this stir-fry – it is light and fresh and helps leaven the richer food served over the Christmas period. Serve it with meat or fish cooked in a ridged pan on the floor of the roasting oven, whilst you cook the broccoli on the boiling plate.

1 teaspoon coriander seeds
450g/1lb broccoli
2 tablespoons sunflower oil
2 tablespoons slivered almonds
1 clove garlic, peeled and crushed
1 teaspoon finely grated ginger
2 tablespoons red wine vinegar
1 tablespoon soy sauce
2 teaspoons sesame oil
1 teaspoon sesame seeds

Put the empty wok on the boiling plate to heat. Lightly crush the coriander seeds in a pestle and mortar. Break the broccoli into small, bite-sized pieces. Pour the sunflower oil into the wok and swirl around. Immediately add the coriander seeds and the almonds and stir-fry for 1 minute, until the nuts are golden brown. Add the garlic, ginger and broccoli and stir-fry for 2 minutes.

Take the wok off the heat and pour on the soy sauce and the sesame oil. Stir well and scatter over the sesame seeds. Serve immediately.

Serves 4

Marinated Courgettes

Courgettes are no longer just a summer vegetable. They keep very well in a cool place, so are a useful vegetable for the holiday period. Serve these courgettes warm as an accompaniment, or cold as a salad, or even as part of an anti-pasti.

4 courgettes, trimmed and thickly sliced
   diagonally
2 tablespoons olive oil

For the dressing
Juice 2 lemons
1 tablespoon chopped mint
1 tablespoon chopped basil leaves
1 clove garlic, peeled and crushed
Salt and pepper

Heat a ridged pan on the floor of the roasting oven for 15 minutes. Brush the courgette slices with a little olive oil. Put the remaining olive oil in a basin and add all the other ingredients. Put a few slices of courgette in the ridged pan and cook for 2-3 minutes on each side. Remove to a plate when just cooked and continue until all the courgettes are cooked.

Whisk the dressing ingredients together and spoon over the warm courgettes and marinate for at least 20 minutes. They can be kept warm resting on the warming plate (of a four-oven Aga) or on top of the boiling plate lid.

Serve warm or cold.

Serves 4-6

Tian of Aubergines

You can serve these aubergines as an accompaniment to cold meat or poultry or, with the addition of some Feta at the end of cooking, as an excellent main dish for vegetarians.

8 tablespoons olive oil
1 red onion, peeled and chopped
2 cloves garlic, peeled and chopped
2 x 400g cans chopped tomatoes
4-5 basil leaves
Salt and pepper
3 aubergines, cut into large dice

Heat one tablespoon of the olive oil in a saucepan and cook the chopped onion until soft but not browning. Add the garlic and cook for 2-3 minutes and then add the tomatoes and the basil leaves. Season. Cover and bring the sauce to the boil. Move to the simmering oven and cook for 30-40 minutes.

Meanwhile, pour 4 tablespoons of the olive oil into a frying pan and sauté half the aubergines until browning. Remove from the pan and drain on kitchen paper. Set aside and cook the remaining aubergine in the remaining 3 tablespoons of olive oil. Butter a shallow ovenproof dish and pour in the tomato sauce. Stir in the drained aubergines.

Hang the shelf on the bottom set of runners of the roasting oven and slide in the dish of aubergines. Bake for 20 minutes and if the aubergines still need further cooking, transfer to the simmering oven for 30 minutes.

Serves 6 as a side dish

Fennel Gratin

Fennel is a much underused and underrated vegetable. It keeps well and so makes a useful standby for the holiday period. Serve this gratin with a simply cooked meat or fish.

2 large bulbs fennel
4 eggs
200ml/7fl oz crème fraîche
6 rounded tablespoons grated Parmesan cheese
Salt and pepper

Trim the root end of the fennel and remove any wilted leaves. Cut each bulb into quarters and remove any hard core. Coarsely grate the fennel (this is most easily done in a food processor if you have one). Beat the eggs and the crème fraîche together in a roomy mixing bowl and stir in the fennel, grated Parmesan and a seasoning of salt and pepper.

Butter a shallow ovenproof dish and pour in the fennel mixture. Sprinkle over the remaining 2 tablespoons of Parmesan cheese. Hang the shelf on the bottom set of runners of the roasting oven and put in the fennel dish. Bake for 25-30 minutes until the mixture is set and golden brown.

Serves 6 as a side dish

Cakes and Puddings

If for the rest of the year you have been good and avoided calorie-heavy cakes and puddings, then this is the time when you are allowed to throw your resolve out of the window and permit yourself to be tempted.

For me, the preparations for Christmas are based around making traditional fruited puddings and cakes. However, I also like to make a few other less traditional but rather special cakes and puddings. So what follows in this chapter are some of my all-time favourites. They include cakes and puddings that are perfect served at any time, such as the Gorgeous Chocolate Cake (page 121), or others that are especially brilliant for entertaining, such as Pavlova (page 126) and Brandy Snaps (page 130). Do, please, also refer to other cakes and pudding recipes in the Cooking in Advance chapter and the Entertaining chapter.

Stollen

This is traditional German Christmas bread, now also very popular here. It can be frozen and then decorated once thawed.

350g/12oz strong white flour
½ teaspoon salt
½ teaspoon ground cinnamon
½ teaspoon mixed spice
50g/2oz butter
1 x 7g sachet easy-blend yeast
25g/1oz caster sugar
175g/6oz luxury mixed dried fruit
50g/2oz whole candied peel, chopped
50g/2oz whole blanched almonds,
    chopped
1 egg, beaten
150ml/¼ pint warm milk
150g/5½oz marzipan
Icing sugar, sieved for decoration

Mix the flour, salt and spices together in a bowl and rub in the butter.
Stir in the yeast and sugar and then all the remaining ingredients except the milk and the marzipan. Mix the dough together with enough milk to make soft but not sticky dough. Turn the dough onto a lightly floured work surface and knead until smooth. Place the dough in a clean bowl and cover with oiled clingfilm.

Place a Chef's Pad or trivet on the boiling plate lid and stand the bowl of stollen mix on top. Leave until doubled in size (about 1 hour). Turn the risen dough onto a floured work surface and lightly knock back. Shape into an elongated oval. Shape the marzipan into a roll just a little shorter than the dough and place down the middle. Fold the dough over the marzipan and press the edges together.

Line a baking tray with Bake-O-Glide and place the stollen on the tray. Cover with oiled clingfilm and return to the top of the Aga boiling plate to rise for about 20-30 minutes. Transfer the baking tray to the bottom set of runners in the roasting oven for 35-40 minutes, until deep brown and sounding hollow when tapped on the bottom. Cool on a wire rack. Dust well with icing sugar.

Traditional Aga Christmas

Glazed Prune Tart

This is one of the easiest puddings you could hope to make and has always proved very popular whenever I have served it to guests. I find it a good idea to keep a jar of prunes topped up with brandy over the Christmas period – they are so versatile and can be enjoyed simply on their own or added to other desserts for a splendidly exotic twist.

1 x 375g packet ready-rolled dessert shortcrust pastry

For the filling
250g/9oz ready-to-eat pitted prunes
5 tablespoons brandy
1 vanilla pod
142ml carton double cream
142ml carton single cream
25g/1oz caster sugar
2 eggs

For the glaze
4 tablespoons apricot jam
2 tablespoons brandy

The day before making the tart place the prunes in a basin and cover with the brandy. Cover and leave to soak overnight or for several hours.

Roll the pastry to line a 23cm/9" loose-bottomed flan tin. Chill. Split the vanilla pod and place in a saucepan with the double cream. Bring to the boil and then remove from the heat and set aside to allow the flavours to infuse. In a bowl, beat together the single cream, caster sugar and the eggs. Remove the vanilla pod from the double cream and pour the infused cream onto the egg mixture. Beat together well.

Drain the prunes and place them in the pastry case. Gently pour over the custard mixture. Put the tart on the floor of the roasting oven to bake. Slide the cold shelf on the second set of runners from the bottom of the roasting oven. Bake for 25-30 minutes, until the pastry is a pale golden colour and the filling is just set.

For the glaze, sieve the jam into a small saucepan and add the brandy. Heat gently, stirring to mix. Use this to glaze the warm tart.

Serves 8

Gorgeous Chocolate Cake

Decorate this wonderfully indulgent cake with foiled chocolate coins for a fun, glittery Christmas look. This cake does not contain flour so should be safe for anyone with a wheat intolerance.

25g/1oz butter
225g/8oz plain chocolate, melted
5 eggs, separated
175g/6oz sugar
125g/5oz ground almonds
2 tablespoons milk
1 teaspoon wine vinegar

For the icing
150g/5$\frac{1}{2}$oz plain chocolate, melted
300ml/$\frac{1}{2}$ pint double cream

Butter and base line a 25 cm/10" spring-release cake tin. Stir the butter into the melted chocolate and remove from the back of the Aga. Whisk the egg whites until white and fluffy. Whisk in the caster sugar, slowly, followed by the egg yolks. Fold in the ground almonds, the chocolate mixture and finally the milk and the wine vinegar. Spoon the mixture carefully into the prepared tin and level the top.

For a two-oven Aga; put the shelf on the floor of the roasting oven. Put in the cake and slide the cold shelf onto the third set of runners from the top of the oven. Bake for 30-40 minutes. For a three- or four-oven Aga; put the shelf on the bottom set of runners of the baking oven and bake the cake for 40-45 minutes. When cooked the cake will be risen and a cake tester or fine skewer inserted in the middle of the cake will come out clean. Leave the cake to cool in the tin.

When the cake is cold and ready for decorating, remove the melted chocolate from the top of the Aga and beat in the cream to form a thick ganache. Stand the cake on a serving plate and spread the top and sides with the ganache. Decorate the top with foil coins or truffles of your own choosing.

Cuts into 8-10 slices

Gateau Pithiviers

This is a traditional French cake from Pithiviers, a town south-west of Paris. It is the custom in France to put one whole almond in the filling – whoever gets the whole nut in their slice of gateau is then crowned King or Queen for the day!

150g/5$\frac{1}{2}$oz butter, softened
150g/5$\frac{1}{2}$oz icing sugar, sieved
2 eggs, beaten
2 tablespoons rum
150g/5$\frac{1}{2}$oz ground almonds
A few drops almond extract
500g/1lb 2oz puff pastry
1 egg, beaten, to glaze

Put the butter and icing sugar in a bowl and beat until light and fluffy. Beat in the eggs and then the rum, ground almonds and the almond extract.

Cut the pastry in half and roll one piece into a circle about 23cm/9" in diameter. Use a plate to trim the edges neatly. Lay the pastry on a baking sheet and spread the filling over the pastry circle, leaving a border of 1cm/$\frac{1}{2}$". Brush the edge with water. Roll a second circle just a little larger than the base piece. Trim and lay it on top of the filling. Seal the edges. Use a sharp knife to score marks to resemble the spokes of a wheel (but do not cut through the pastry). Knock up the edges. Brush the top well with beaten egg.

To bake, hang the baking tray on the third set of runners from the top of the roasting oven for 20-30 minutes until a rich, golden brown. Serve freshly baked and warm.

Serves 10-12

Buche de Noel

Buche de Noel is a rich chocolate log filled with chestnut purée. You can make and freeze it in advance. Freeze on a tray and then wrap to prevent spoiling the decoration. Unwrap before thawing.

6 eggs, separated
150g/5$\frac{1}{2}$oz caster sugar
50g/2oz cocoa powder

For the filling
440g/15$\frac{1}{2}$oz can chestnut purée
150ml/$\frac{1}{4}$ pint double cream

For the topping
300ml/$\frac{1}{2}$ pint double cream
100g/3$\frac{1}{2}$oz plain chocolate, melted
Icing sugar

Line a large roasting tin or baking tray with a sheet of Bake-O-Glide.

Whisk the egg whites until white and fluffy. Put the egg yolks and caster sugar in a mixing bowl and whisk together until thick and pale. Whisk in the cocoa powder. Beat in 1 tablespoon of whisked egg white to slacken the mixture and then fold in the remaining egg white. Spoon the mixture carefully into the lined tin and gently level off.

Hang the tin on the bottom set of runners of the roasting oven and bake for 8-10 minutes, until firm when lightly touched. Remove from the oven and set aside to cool.

Mash down the chestnut purée and then gradually beat in the cream.

Turn the roulade onto a plain sheet of Bake-O-Glide and peel off the lining sheet. Spread the chestnut purée over. Roll the roulade into a tight roll, with the longest side nearest you. Roll onto a serving plate and have the edge tucked underneath to prevent the roulade from rolling off the plate.

Stir the cream into the melted chocolate to thicken. Spread the topping over the chocolate roll. Using a knife and fork, decorate to look like a log. Allow it to set. Dust with sieved icing sugar to create a look of snow.

Serves 10-12

Buche de Noel, page 123

Pavlova

Pavlova is always a popular dessert. It looks so impressive, and you can vary the type of fruit you choose for the topping each time you make one. Some people like a very soft meringue, whilst others like it dry – the choice is yours. But if you plan to make the meringue in advance, then it will need to be as dry as possible for storage.

4 egg whites
225g/8oz caster sugar
1 teaspoon cornflour
1 teaspoon white wine vinegar

For the topping
300ml/$^{1}\!/_{2}$ pint double cream
A selection of fresh fruits such as mango,
    raspberries, pineapple, blueberries,
    passion fruits, physallis

Line the cold shelf with a sheet of Bake-O-Glide. Put the egg whites into the large bowl of an electric mixer. Mix the caster sugar and cornflour together. Whisk the egg whites until white and forming peaks. Keep the mixer whisking and add the sugar and cornflour mixture, no more than 1 teaspoon at a time. When all the sugar has been whisked in, sprinkle over the vinegar and fold in. Spoon the meringue onto the lined tray in a large circle. Use the back of the spoon to form small peaks all over the meringue.

Put the pavlova in the middle of the simmering oven and leave to dry for 3-4 hours, until the meringue is crisp on the outside but has some softness inside. Remove from the oven and cool on a wire rack.

Whisk the cream until soft peaks start to form. Stand the pavlova on a serving plate and spoon the whipped cream on top, leaving a border of meringue. Pile on a selection of fruits.

Serves 6-8

Rich Sticky Gingerbread

This is an enriched version of the gingerbread to be found in my first book, *The Traditional Aga Cookery Book*. I have tried many alternatives over the years, but in the end always come back to this one. At Christmas time I add crystallised ginger to the basic recipe, which gives it a nice seasonal edge.

300ml/$\frac{1}{2}$ pint milk
2 level teaspoons bicarbonate of soda
350g/12oz plain flour
2 level teaspoons ground ginger
2 level teaspoons ground cinnamon
225g/8oz butter
225g/8oz soft brown sugar
110g/4oz golden syrup
110g/4oz treacle
2 eggs
6 balls crystallised ginger, finely chopped

Line the small roasting tin with Bake-O-Glide. Measure the milk into a jug and add the bicarbonate of soda, stand on the back of the Aga to warm. Sieve the flour, ginger and cinnamon into a large mixing bowl. Put the butter, sugar, golden syrup and treacle in a saucepan and stand on the simmering plate. Heat and stir until the butter has melted. Remove from the heat and pour into the flour and spices. Mix together well and then beat in the eggs, one at a time. Next, stir in the warmed milk mixture followed by the crystallised ginger. Pour the gingerbread batter into the prepared tin. Bake.

For a two-oven Aga; hang the roasting tin on the bottom set of runners of the roasting oven and put the cold shelf on the third set of runners from the top of the oven. For a three- or four-oven Aga; hang the roasting tin on the second set of runners from the bottom of the baking oven. Bake the gingerbread for 30-40 minutes until risen and a cake tester or fine skewer inserted in the middle come out clean. Cool and store in the tin. This gingerbread is at its best a day or two after baking.

Brandy Snaps

These crunchy little biscuits can be served on their own, just rolled and filled with whipped cream. Or, instead of biscuits, the mixture can be formed into baskets to be filled with fruit or mousse. The snaps can be made a few days ahead of serving, but must be stored in an airtight container until ready to serve.

50g/2oz butter
50g/2oz caster sugar
2 tablespoons golden syrup
50g/2oz plain flour
$\frac{1}{2}$ level teaspoon ground ginger
Finely grated rind $\frac{1}{2}$ lemon

Line the cold shelf or large baking tray with Bake-O-Glide. Put the butter, sugar and syrup in a saucepan and stand on the simmering plate, stirring until the butter has melted and the sugar dissolved. Remove from the heat. Sieve the flour and ginger together and stir into the melted mixture along with the lemon rind. Drop 4 teaspoons of mixture onto the lined tray, allowing enough room for the mixture to spread.

Hang the tray on the bottom set of runners of the roasting oven and bake for 6-7 minutes, until thinly spread out and a golden colour. Whilst baking, butter the handle of a wooden spoon to make snaps or grease the base of an inverted ramekin if you want to shape into baskets.

Remove the snaps quickly from the baking tray and roll around the spoon handle or drape over the ramekin or just place on a wire rack. Shape the snaps while still pliable and then cool on the wire rack. If the snaps set before shaping, return them to the oven for a minute to soften. Repeat, using up all the mixture.

The subsequent batches may cook more quickly as the baking tray gets warmer. Fill with fruit, cream or mousse just before serving.

Makes 12

Caramel Oranges

This is a refreshing dessert making the most of the seasonal citrus fruits. Any size of orange can be used, although satsumas and tangerines look particularly attractive left whole. Prepare these fruits several hours before eating to allow the fruit to chill and the flavours to develop.

175g/6oz granulated sugar
450ml/15fl oz water
6 large oranges or 12 tangerines, peeled of all white pith

To make the caramel, put the sugar into a saucepan with half the water and stand on the simmering plate. Allow the sugar to dissolve, but without stirring or allowing the water to boil. When the sugar has dissolved, allow the mixture to boil and to turn a pale golden colour. Watch the mixture, it will turn black very quickly!

Lift the pan from the heat and pour in the remaining water, be careful, it may spit. Return to the heat and stir to make a caramel syrup. When the caramel is dissolved, remove from the heat. Slice the oranges horizontally into slices, removing any pips (or separate the tangerine segments) and lay them out in a serving dish. Pour on the caramel and cover. Allow to stand for at least 8 hours.

Serves 4

Mini Cranberry and Walnut Muffins

These seasonal little muffins are at their best when served straight from the oven.

75g/3oz butter
200g/7oz plain flour
$\frac{1}{2}$ teaspoon bicarbonate of soda
2 teaspoons baking powder
100g/3$\frac{1}{2}$oz caster sugar
1 egg, beaten
200ml/7fl oz buttermilk or plain yoghurt
150g/5$\frac{1}{2}$oz cranberries
100g/3$\frac{1}{2}$oz walnuts, chopped

Line 2 mini muffin trays with paper mini muffin cases. Put the butter in a basin and stand at the back of the Aga to melt. In a large bowl, mix together the flour, bicarbonate of soda, the baking powder and the caster sugar.

Beat the egg, buttermilk or yoghurt and the melted butter together. Mix the liquid with the dry ingredients and stir in briskly but do take care not to over mix. Stir in the cranberries and walnuts. Spoon teaspoons of mixture into the paper cases.

Hang the shelf on the third set of runners from the top of the roasting oven and slide in the muffin tins. Bake the muffins for 12-14 minutes, until risen, golden brown and firm to the touch. Cool on a wire rack. Repeat with the remaining mixture. The muffins can be frozen.

Makes about 48

Entertaining

Most of us love to entertain at Christmas (and some of us, of course, love to be entertained). Drinks parties seem to be the most popular way, whether with the local carol singers, the neighbours or just close friends.

Small nibbles can be time-consuming to prepare, so I have come up with some ideas in this chapter that aren't too fiddly. One of the secrets is to serve the nibbles so that they look both stunning and plentiful. Hunt around the house and see what you can find that will help make the food look great when served – mirrors and prettily decorated trays always look effective. Or choose a simple colour theme, and don't worry if the serving plates are all different shapes. Arrange canapés in rows or circles on the platters, but take care not to overcrowd them.

As a rule of thumb, allow 10 canapés per person. If you don't have a supply of helpers handing around the food, then hand out small plates and napkins so that two or three pieces can be taken at a time. Remember to have somewhere for guests to discard used cocktail sticks and, if necessary, a few finger bowls to dip sticky fingers into.

But whatever else you do, be sure not to spend all your time stuck in the kitchen!

Mini Roast Beef Yorkshire Puddings

These exquisite little Yorkshire puddings are made in mini-muffin tins and then topped with thin slices of fillet steak and horseradish sauce – they are quite delicious!

1 tablespoon vegetable oil
1 egg
110g/4oz plain flour
Pinch salt
150ml/5fl oz milk
225g/8oz fillet steak
110g/4oz horseradish sauce

Put a little oil in two 12 portion mini-muffin tins. Stand the trays on the floor of the roasting oven and allow to heat while making the batter. Put the flour and salt in a bowl. Add the egg and a little of the milk and using a balloon whisk start whisking the egg and milk into the flour. Add more milk to make a smooth batter, the consistency of thick double cream.

Remove the smoking hot trays from the oven and pour the batter into the tins. Hang the shelf on the third set of runners from the top of the roasting oven and put in the Yorkshire puddings. Bake for 20-25 minutes, until risen and golden. Remove the puddings from the oven and set aside to cool.

Meanwhile, heat a ridged pan on the floor of the roasting oven for 15-20 minutes. When hot put the pan on the boiling plate and cook the fillet steak for 3-4 minutes on each side, depending upon the thickness of the steak. The steak will be at its best if left pink in the middle. Remove the meat from the pan and leave to rest for 5 minutes before slicing very thinly.

Assemble the puddings no more than an hour before serving. Place them on a serving plate and spoon a scant teaspoon of horseradish sauce onto each one and top with a strip of the beef.

Makes 24

Spiced Potato Wedges

Serve these potato wedges with a refreshing dip of soured cream or crème fraîche.

2 large Desirée potatoes
2 tablespoons olive oil
2 level tablespoons Jamaican jerk
  seasoning
Soured cream, to dip
1 lime cut into wedges, to garnish

Scrub the potatoes, but do not peel. Cut lengthways into thin wedges and pat dry with kitchen paper. In a large bowl, mix together the oil and jerk seasoning. Add the potato wedges and toss very well in the seasoned oil until completely coated. Line a large baking tray with Bake-O-Glide and spread out the potatoes in a single layer.

Hang the tin on the second set of runners from the top of the roasting oven and bake until the potatoes are crisp and golden brown, about 25-30 minutes. Part way through cooking give them a shake and a stir and turn the tray round if they are browning more on one side than the other. Tip onto kitchen paper to mop up any excess oil. Serve hot with the soured cream dip and lime wedges to squeeze over, if liked. The wedges can be prepared and tossed in the seasoned oil an hour or two before cooking, but be sure to serve them fresh from the oven.

Parsnip Spikes

6 small parsnips
2-3 tablespoons olive oil

Peel the parsnips, remove the cores and cut into 4, lengthways. Cut each quarter again to make 8 strips from each parsnip. Put the parsnips in a bowl and pour on some olive oil, toss well and then lay the parsnips on a baking tray lined with Bake-O-Glide.

Hang the tray on the third set of runners from the top of the roasting oven and cook the parsnips until golden brown and tender, about 20-25 minutes. Do keep an eye on them towards the end of the cooking time as parsnips have a tendency to burn. Put the cooked parsnip spikes in a serving dish and scatter over a few salt flakes.

Serves 6

Sesame Seed Tarts with Smoked Salmon Mousse

These sesame seed tartlet cases can be used for a variety of fillings. They can be made several hours in advance or even frozen raw and then freshly baked.

250g/8oz plain flour
110g/4oz butter, diced
50g/2oz Parmesan cheese, grated
1 tablespoon toasted sesame seeds
1 egg

For the Salmon Mousse
300g/10$\frac{1}{2}$oz cream cheese
1 teaspoon mustard
Rind and juice $\frac{1}{2}$ lemon
1 teaspoon chopped dill
110g/4oz cooked smoked salmon
2 pieces smoked salmon, cut into thin
   strips to garnish

You will need three 12-hole mini-muffin tins.

Place the flour in a bowl and add the butter. Rub the butter into the flour until it resembles breadcrumbs. Stir in the cheese and the sesame seeds. Beat the egg and add to the pastry mixture. Stir to combine the pastry, adding a little cold water if needed. Draw the pastry together and knead lightly. Allow it to rest for 5 minutes and then roll out to the thickness of a £1 coin.

Stamp out 36 rounds and line the tins. Chill for 30 minutes. Bake the pastry cases on the floor of the roasting oven for 10-15 minutes until dry and golden. Cool for 2-3 minutes in the tin and then take out of the tins and put on a serving plate.

To make the salmon mousse, put the cream cheese in a bowl and beat well to slacken. Add the mustard, lemon juice, rind and dill and beat well. Flake the salmon and fold into the cream cheese mixture. Use this to fill the cooled pastry cases. Garnish with a twisted strip of smoked salmon and a tiny sprig of dill.

Makes 36

Sesame Seed Tarts
with Smoked Salmon Mousse

Smoked salmon is such a traditional staple
at this time of year, often making a classic starter
or perfect breakfast for Christmas Day. This is an
easy and very tasty alternative recipe.

Sesame seed tarts with smoked salmon mousse, page 139

Pastry Squares with Ricotta and Tomato

I particularly like these tasty little pastry squares as they are very quick and easy to make and so versatile – just vary the topping to suit personal preferences.

375g pack ready-rolled puff pastry
  (from the chilled compartment)
100g/3$\frac{1}{2}$oz Ricotta cheese
2 teaspoons sun-dried tomato paste
20 cherry tomatoes

Unroll the pastry. Cut the pastry into 20 squares and lay the squares onto a large baking tray lined with a sheet of Bake-O-Glide. Mix together the Ricotta cheese and the sun-dried tomato paste. Spoon a little mixture into the middle of each square. Put one tomato half, cut side up, and one half cut side down, on top of the ricotta mixture.

Hang the tin on the third set of runners from the top of the roasting oven for 15 minutes and then transfer to the floor of the roasting oven for a further 5 minutes to crisp the pastry bases. The pastries should be risen and golden brown and can be served warm or cold.

Makes 20

Traditional Aga Christmas

Bruschetta

Bruschetta is brilliantly simple to make. You can toast the bread several days in advance and, once cold, store in tins or plastic bags. Different sizes can be made according to the shape of bread that you choose, while a whole variety and style of toppings can be used. You will need to buy a loaf that, when cut, every piece ends up having a crust – this will help to hold the bruschetta together when the topping is put on.

1 baguette
Jar of olive tapenade
375g/13oz goats' cheese log, cut into thin
   slices

Slice the bread and lay the slices on a baking tray. Hang the tray on the second set of runners from the top of the roasting oven and toast the bread until golden brown. Do keep an eye on the bread during this time to ensure that it doesn't burn. Turn the toasted bread over and spread 1-2 teaspoons of tapenade over each slice of toast. Put a slice of cheese on top of the tapenade. Return the tray to the third set of runners from the top of the roasting oven and cook until the cheese is bubbling (about 5-8 minutes).

Spiced Nuts

Spiced nuts make good drinks nibbles (and also keep very well in jars). The selection of nuts you choose can be varied to suit taste and availability.

2 tablespoons olive oil
$\frac{1}{2}$ teaspoon ground cumin
$\frac{1}{2}$ teaspoon ground coriander
$\frac{1}{4}$ teaspoon chilli powder
$\frac{1}{4}$ teaspoon ground ginger
$\frac{1}{4}$ teaspoon ground cinnamon
75g/2$\frac{3}{4}$oz pecans
75g/2$\frac{3}{4}$oz cashews
225g/8oz almonds, skin on
Sea salt

Heat the oil in a frying pan on the simmering plate and add the spices.

Stir and cook the spices gently for 2-3 minutes, taking care not to burn them. Add the nuts and stir until well coated with the spice mixture. Tip the nuts onto a baking tray lined with Bake-O-Glide.

Hang the tin in the middle of the simmering oven for 15-20 minutes, or until golden. Sprinkle with salt and cool.

These nuts can be stored but make sure they are completely cold before putting in a jar with a fitted lid.

Devils on Horseback

The classic combination of prunes and bacon is delicious and always proves popular at parties. Even those who say they don't like prunes love these little beauties. They are, however, slightly fiddly to make, but can be prepared up to 24 hours in advance and kept chilled until ready for cooking.

12 rashers good, thinly cut, streaky bacon
24 ready-to-eat prunes
24 cocktail sticks

Cut the bacon rashers in half, lengthways. Wrap a piece of bacon round each prune and secure with a skewer or cocktail stick. Lay each wrapped prune on a baking tray lined with Bake-O-Glide.

To cook, hang the tin on the second set of runners from the top of the roasting oven and cook for 15 minutes, then turn over and cook for a further 5 minutes until the bacon is crisp.

Makes 24

" Most of us love to entertain at Christmas (and some of us, of course, love to be entertained).

But whatever else you do,
be sure not to spend all
your time stuck in the
kitchen!"

Smoked Mackerel or Hot Smoked Salmon Dip

Home-made dips are easy to make and so much nicer than anything you can buy.

250g / 9 oz smoked fish, use either
   smoked mackerel or hot smoked
   salmon
200g / 7 oz cream cheese
1 lemon, finely grated zest and juice
2 tablespoons creamed horseradish
1 tablespoon chopped parsley
1 tablespoon chopped chives

Skin, bone and flake the fish on to a plate. Put the cream cheese into a mixing bowl and beat well to soften. Add the lemon zest and juice and the creamed horseradish and beat together well.

Fold in the flaked fish, parsley and chives. Spoon into a serving dish and cover with cling film. Stand somewhere cool for at least an hour to allow the flavours to develop.

Serve with olive oil crackers (opposite).

Olive Oil Crackers

These versatile crackers can be made to the size that best suits your occasion.
Make a day or two in advance and store in an airtight container.

250g/9oz plain flour
1 level teaspoon baking powder
115ml/4 fl oz water
2 tablespoons olive oil, plus a little for
    brushing
Generous pinch salt
1 level teaspoon paprika
Generous pinch cayenne pepper
Grinding black pepper
Salt flakes, to sprinkle

Put all the ingredients except the salt flakes into a mixing bowl and knead together to form a soft dough consistency. If preferred, this can be done with a mixer and dough hook.

Cover with cling film and chill in the fridge for 1 hour.

Line a large baking tray with Bake-O-Glide.

Cut the dough into walnut-sized pieces and roll each piece on a lightly floured worktop as thinly as possible to a long thin shape, or a shape of your choice. Place the crackers on the lined baking tray. Brush each cracker with plenty of olive oil and sprinkle lightly with salt flakes. Slide the baking tray on to the second set of runners from the top of the roasting oven and bake for 5-6 minutes until crisp and golden.

Serve warm from the oven. Alternatively, leave to become completely cold and place in an airtight container. They should stay fresh for up to two days.

Makes about 25

Thai Fishcakes with Cucumber Relish

Make these delicious little fishcakes in well-greased mini-muffin tins. To slip them out easily and for attractive serving I like to put paper cases in each tin.

For the Cucumber Relish
150ml/5fl oz rice vinegar
50g/2oz caster sugar
1/4 cucumber
1/4 red onion
1 small red chilli

Put the vinegar and sugar into a saucepan. Stand on the simmering plate and heat to allow the sugar to dissolve. Bring to the boil and then remove from the heat. Cool. Cut the cucumber in half lengthways and remove the seeds. Chop into fine dice. Peel and finely chop the onion. Remove the seeds from the chilli and finely chop. Place the prepared vegetables in a serving dish and pour on the rice vinegar syrup. Serve as a dip for the fish cakes.

For the Thai Fishcakes
500g/1lb 2oz firm white fish, such as cod, roughly chopped
1 tablespoon sugar
50ml/2fl oz fish sauce
1 tablespoon Thai red curry paste
1/4 red pepper, finely chopped
1/4 green pepper, finely chopped

Grease or line three 12 portion mini-muffin tins. Put the fish, sugar and fish sauce in a food processor and chop to a smooth purée. Add the curry paste and whiz to combine. Tip the mixture into a bowl and mix in the chopped peppers. Spoon a teaspoonful of the mixture into each muffin tin. Hang the oven shelf onto the bottom set of runners of the roasting oven and put in the fishcakes. Bake for 12-15 minutes, until lightly browned. Remove from the tins and serve with the cucumber relish.

Makes 36

Chilli Salt Squid

These tasty oriental rings have converted many doubters to squid. They are so easy to prepare and so sublimely irresistible that you may want to double the recipe quantity. They can be served hot or cold.

300g/10½oz squid, cleaned, dried and cut into rings
Cornflour for dusting
2 teaspoons salt
1 teaspoon Chinese five-spice
Freshly ground black pepper
6 tablespoons sunflower oil for frying

Toss the squid rings in the cornflour. Mix together the salt, Chinese five-spice and a good grind of pepper. Put to one side.

Pour the oil into a wok and heat through on the boiling plate. When hot, drop in the squid rings, one at a time and fry until crisp and golden. Cook in batches to ensure the squid crisps quickly. Remove from the pan and drain on kitchen paper. When all the squid is cooked, tip into a bowl and pour over the spice mixture and toss well. Serve.

Pesto Palmiers

These pretty pastries can be prepared in advance and then baked freshly just before serving. I have used quite an elaborate filling in this recipe but you could just as successfully use Marmite and finely grated Cheddar cheese!

375g packet ready-rolled puff pastry
3-4 tablespoons good quality green pesto
4 tablespoons finely grated Parmesan
   cheese

Unroll the pastry onto a work surface. Spread the pesto evenly all over the surface of the pastry and scatter over the Parmesan cheese. Cut the pastry in half, lengthways. Roll the narrow end nearest to you in a tight roll into the middle. Turn the pastry round and roll the end nearest to you in a tight roll to the middle where it should meet the other roll. Chill for at least 30 minutes. Repeat with the remaining sheet of pastry. Slice through across the rolls so that each 1.5cm/^{3}/$_4$ inch piece has two little swirls either end.

Place the palmiers, cut side down, on a baking tray lined with Bake-O-Glide. Bake on the third set of runners from the top of the roasting oven for 15-20 minutes or until golden brown.

Makes approximately 40

Chocolate Tea Pots

Serve these chocolate delights in pretty espresso cups. They are very rich, so only a little is needed!

125g/4½oz dark chocolate, at least 70% cocoa content
400ml/14fl oz single cream
1 tablespoon Earl Grey tea leaves
1 teaspoon orange flower water

Finely chop the chocolate and put in a heatproof bowl.

Scald the cream by bringing it to the boil. Add the tea to the cream and leave it to infuse for 2 minutes. Strain.

Pour the cream gently onto the chocolate, stirring to make a smooth emulsion. If the chocolate is not melting, stand the bowl at the back of the Aga just long enough to soften the chocolate. Add the orange flower water.

Pour into small coffee cups and chill for 2 hours.

Serves 8

Cranberry and Marzipan Plait

This delicious dessert combines two of the classic ingredients of Christmas, cranberries and marzipan. It is also both impressive to look at and surprisingly easy to make.

375g packet ready-rolled puff pastry
450g cranberries
250g marzipan
1 egg, beaten to glaze
Icing sugar for dusting

Rinse the cranberries and remove any stalks and bruised ones. Place in a saucepan, cover and stand on the simmering plate. Simmer until the cranberries are just cooked and have finished popping. Tip into a bowl and leave them to become cold.

Unroll the pastry and lay on a sheet of Bake-O-Glide. Roll out the marzipan to the length of the pastry roll and 10cm / 4" wide. Place in the middle of the pastry sheet. Spoon the cold cranberries on to the marzipan.

Cut 2.5cm /1" wide strips at an angle of 45degrees from 1cm / ½ " from the edge of the marzipan to the edge of the pastry. Cut the same number of strips on each side of the plait. Brush the cut strips with beaten egg. Overlap alternate strips from side to side over the cranberries to form a plait. Brush with beaten egg.

Lift the plait still on the sheet of Bake-O-Glide on to a large baking tray. Place the tray on the third set of runners from the top of the roasting oven. Bake for 15-20 minutes until risen and golden brown. Move the baking tray to the floor of the roasting oven for 5 minutes to crisp the base.

Lift the plait on to a serving plate or board and dust with icing sugar.

The plait can be made and frozen before baking. Thaw for 30 minutes and bake as per instructions. It may need a few minutes longer in the oven.

Petits Fours

These little biscuits are ideal to hand around as something sweet with drinks or with coffee. They also make lovely presents if wrapped prettily.

2 egg whites
110g/4oz ground almonds
110g/4oz caster sugar
4 drops almond essence
Glacé cherries, quartered

Line a large baking tray with Bake-O-Glide. Whisk the egg whites until stiff. Scatter over the ground almonds and the caster sugar and fold carefully into the egg whites, along with the almond essence. Spoon the mixture into a large piping bag fitted with a star nozzle. Pipe stars onto the baking tray, allowing a little room for the mixture to spread. Add to each star a piece of glacé cherry.

To bake in a two-oven Aga; hang the tray on the bottom set of runners of the roasting oven and slide in the cold shelf two runners above. Bake for 20 minutes. For a three- and four-oven Aga; hang the tray on the second set of runners from the bottom of the baking oven and bake for 20-25 minutes.

The petits fours will be a pale golden brown when cooked. Cool on a wire rack.

Makes about 24

Petits fours, page 157

Christmas Leftovers

One of the great pleasures at Christmas is being able to eat up all the delicious leftovers. I have even been known to eat leftover trifle for breakfast on Boxing Day! It's important to store leftovers carefully, especially any meat or fish, which should be covered and then refrigerated as soon as they have cooled.

I have included all the usual favourites here, such as Bubble and Squeak Cakes (page 169) and a wonderful Turkey and Ham Soup (page 162). Stock and soups can be made from the meat carcass with little effort in the Aga. Cheese can be grated and frozen ready for use later. Leftover cream can be stirred into soups and added to a quiche filling, or alternatively stirred into rice pudding to make it absolutely divine.

I like to store leftover mincemeat for use during the dull winter months that follow, as it keeps very well in a cool place. It is excellent when used to stuff baked apples or when added to cakes or flapjacks. At Christmas we are all guilty of buying too many nuts, so why not make a delicious Nut Loaf (page 62) or stir some into homemade muesli, which is so simple to make and very healthy. Remember that nuts and biscuits can be successfully refreshed in the simmering oven.

Creamed Turkey and Ham Soup

This soup is wonderful using the stock made from the turkey carcass. If you don't have any ham left, then just serve creamed turkey soup!

For the stock
1 turkey carcass, broken up
3 sticks celery, roughly chopped
3 leeks, washed and chopped
1 carrot, washed and chopped
2 onions, peeled and roughly chopped
3 cloves garlic, peeled and crushed
2 bay leaves
2-3 sprigs fresh thyme
6 peppercorns
6 sprigs parsley

For the soup
3 generous tablespoons long-grain rice
150ml/$\frac{1}{4}$ pint double cream
150g/5$\frac{1}{2}$oz cooked turkey meat, diced
200g/7oz cooked ham, diced
2 tablespoons chopped fresh parsley
Juice $\frac{1}{2}$ lemon
Salt and pepper

Put all the stock ingredients into a large saucepan. Just cover with water. Cover with a lid and stand on the boiling plate and bring to the boil. Boil well for 2-3 minutes and then move the pan to the simmering oven. Allow the stock to cook for 3-4 hours. Strain the stock well, discarding all the solid bone and vegetables. Pour the strained stock into a large pan and bring to the boil. Skim off any scum. If necessary, reduce the stock by boiling to intensify the flavour.

Pour the rice into the stock, bring to the boil and then transfer to the simmering oven for 30-40 minutes, until the rice is very well cooked. Spoon the stock into a blender and whiz until smooth. Return to the saucepan and stir in the cream, the diced turkey and ham. Warm through on the simmering plate for 5 minutes. Add the parsley and lemon juice. Adjust the seasoning.

Serves 6-8

Turkey Pastries

You can make these brilliant pastries any size that you like, though you will find that 2 or 3 smaller triangles will look far nicer than one large one.

For the filling
25g/1oz butter
175g/6oz mushrooms, wiped and finely
  chopped
4 rashers bacon, rind removed, finely
  diced
350g/12oz cooked turkey meat, finely
  shredded
150g/5 $^{1}/_{2}$oz cream cheese
2 spring onions, trimmed and finely sliced
Salt and pepper

For the pastry wrapping
50g/2oz butter
24 sheets filo pastry

Heat the butter in a frying pan and add the mushrooms and the bacon. Cook over a high heat until the mushrooms are cooked and no juices are left in the pan. Remove from the heat and tip into a bowl. Add the turkey, cream cheese and the spring onions. Mix gently, but thoroughly. Season.

Unroll the pastry and brush the top layer with melted butter. Place on the worktop and lay a second plain sheet of pastry on top. Brush with butter and lay the third sheet on top. Butter. Cut the pastry sheet into three long strips. Place a tablespoon of turkey mixture at one end of the strip. Fold the end where the filling is diagonally across to form a triangle enclosing the filling. Continue folding the length of the filo strip. Repeat using all the pastry and filling.

Line a baking tray with Bake-O-Glide and place the triangles on the tray. Brush with the remaining melted butter. Hang the baking tray on the third set of runners of the roasting oven and bake for 20-25 minutes, until the triangles are golden.

Makes about 24

Turkey or Chicken Tatin

This is one of my favourite ways to prepare leftover pieces of turkey – it's a little different from the usual turkey pie with a sauce!

2 tablespoons olive oil
1 onion, peeled and finely sliced
3 cloves garlic, peeled and finely sliced
450g/1lb cooked turkey or chicken meat
2 tablespoons green pesto
Salt and pepper
1 x 375g pack ready-rolled puff pastry
Rocket leaves or watercress, to garnish
Parmesan shavings, to garnish

Pour the olive oil in the base of a 23cm/9" pie tin or ovenproof dish. Lay the onions over the base in a single layer and scatter over the slices of garlic. Slice the cooked poultry finely and place in a mixing bowl. Add the pesto and stir together. Lay the chicken or turkey slices over the onions and season with salt and pepper.

Unroll the pastry; you will need a piece the same diameter as the tin and so may find you need to lightly roll out the pastry for it to fit. Lay the pastry over the chicken and tuck in the edges.

Place the tin directly on the floor of the roasting oven for 20-25 minutes, until the pastry is risen and golden brown. Leave the tatin to set for 2-3 minutes before inverting onto a plate. Top the tatin with the leaves and the shavings of Parmesan.

Serves 4-6

Salmon Fishcakes with Lemon Butter Sauce

The lemon butter sauce in this recipe is a delicious addition to one of my favourite leftover dishes.

350g/12oz salmon fillet, cooked
350g/12oz cooked and mashed potato
1 tablespoon tomato ketchup
1 teaspoon mustard
2 tablespoons finely chopped parsley
Plain flour
1 tablespoon olive oil
25g/1oz butter

For the Lemon Butter Sauce
3 tablespoons lemon juice
40g/1½oz butter
125ml/¼ pint double cream
2 tablespoons finely chopped chives
Salt and pepper

Flake the cooked salmon, removing any skin and bone. In a mixing bowl, add half the salmon to the potato, tomato ketchup, mustard and parsley. Mix well together and season with salt and pepper. Add the remaining salmon and mix in, but take care to keep the salmon unbroken. Divide into 6 even-sized portions. Flour your hands and shape each portion into a fishcake. Chill for at least half an hour.

Using a frying pan that can fit into the oven, heat the butter and the olive oil and put in the fishcakes. Put the pan on the floor of the roasting oven and cook for about 5 minutes. They should be golden on the underside. Turn over and cook for a further 10 minutes, until crisp and heated through.

To make the lemon butter sauce, melt the butter in a saucepan, add the cream and heat through. Whisk in the lemon juice and chives, taking care not to boil the sauce. Adjust the seasoning. Serve with the fishcakes.

Serves 6

Salmon Soufflé

This is a really good way to use up leftover salmon. Soufflés can be prepared and mixed an hour before cooking – just make sure that those who are going to enjoy the soufflé are at the table when it comes out of the oven! Don't fret about opening the oven door during the cooking time – I have been known to take a soufflé out of the oven and return it to a different position to no ill effect at all.

200ml/7fl oz milk
1 small carrot, peeled and sliced
1 small onion, peeled and sliced
1 bay leaf
6 black peppercorns
50g/1³⁄₄oz plain flour
25g/1oz butter
Salt and pepper
110g/4oz cooked salmon, flaked
4 eggs, separated

Butter a 1.3 litre/2 ¹⁄₄ pint soufflé dish.

Put the milk in a saucepan and add the carrot, onion, bay leaf and peppercorns. Bring to the boil and then remove from the heat and leave to infuse for 30 minutes. Strain the milk and discard the vegetables and the bay leaves and peppercorns. Return the milk to the rinsed-out pan and add the flour and the butter. Stand the pan on the simmering plate and whisk all the ingredients together until a smooth, glossy sauce has been made. Season with salt and pepper and then beat in the egg yolks one at a time. Fold in the flaked salmon.

Whisk the egg whites until white and stiff. Beat 1 tablespoon of egg white into the sauce. Then pour the sauce over the remaining egg white and gently fold the two together. Spoon the soufflé mixture into the buttered dish. Wipe the rim of the dish clean, this allows the soufflé to rise well without snagging.

Put the shelf on the floor of the roasting oven and put in the soufflé. Bake for 25-30 minutes at which point the soufflé should be risen, golden brown and firm to the touch on the sides. Serve immediately.

Serves 4

Cheesey
Bubble and Squeak Cakes

Making bubble and squeak is one of the most popular ways of using up leftover vegetables. If you don't have any, you can of course use freshly cooked vegetables.

700g/1¹⁄₂lb potatoes, peeled and cut into large dice
350g/12oz swede, peeled and diced
1 large leek, trimmed and shredded
225g/8oz cabbage, finely shredded
1 tablespoon vegetable oil
1 large carrot, peeled and grated
1 egg yolk
250g/9oz Raclette or Gruyère cheese, cut into 4 cubes
1 tablespoon flour
4 tablespoons oil

Put the peeled and diced potato and swede into a saucepan and add enough water to come 2.5cm/1" up the side of the saucepan. Season with salt, cover and bring to the boil. Boil for one minute and then drain. Re-cover the pan and put the vegetables in the simmering oven for 30 minutes, or until the vegetables are soft enough to mash. Drain off any excess water and roughly mash the vegetables.

Heat one tablespoon of the oil in a large sauté pan. Fry the leek and the cabbage and cook until softening, but not browning. Add the carrot, mashed potato and swede. Remove from the heat and add the egg yolk. Divide the mixture into 4 equal portions.

Wet your hands and flatten a portion of the potato mixture and place a portion of cheese in the middle. Mould the potato mixture around the cheese. Shape into a neat cake and dust with flour. Make the remaining cakes in the same way. Heat 2 tablespoons of the oil in a frying pan on the floor of the roasting oven. Add the bubble and squeak cakes and cook until brown. Turn over and cook the other side, adding more oil if needed. This will take about 10 minutes in all. Serve immediately so that the cheese oozes when the bubble and squeak cakes are cut.

Serves 4

Ham and Cheese Jalousie

This is an excellent and simple way to use up any leftover pieces of ham. Although I have given specific quantities in this recipe, feel free to add as much ham and cheese as you like.

1 x packet ready-rolled puff pastry
2-3 teaspoons grainy mustard
175g/6oz ham slices
110g/4oz Cheddar cheese, grated
1 egg, to glaze

Unroll the pastry and cut in half. Lay one sheet on a baking tray. Spread this sheet of pastry with the mustard, leaving a border round the edge. Lay over the slices of ham, leaving the border clear. Sprinkle over the grated cheese. Lay the remaining piece of pastry on a worktop and cut strips through the centre of the pastry,

leaving a border to keep the sheet of pastry intact. Carefully lay the pastry lid on top. Seal the edges and decorate them. Glaze with the beaten egg.

Bake on the second set of runners from the top of the roasting oven for 15 minutes and then put the tray on the floor of the oven for a further 5 minutes.

Serve immediately.

Serves 6

Mincemeat Flapjacks

Flapjacks are so easy to make – easy enough for even young children to prepare. And the perfect way to use up those jars of mincemeat left lingering in the cupboard.

425g/15oz porridge oats
225g/8oz mincemeat
175g/6oz butter
300g/11oz golden syrup

Line the small roasting tin with Bake-O-Glide.

Measure the oats into a roomy mixing bowl. Measure the mincemeat, butter and golden syrup into a saucepan and stand on the simmering plate. Stir the contents of the pan until the butter has melted. Pour the melted mixture into the oats and stir until all the oats are coated with the syrup mixture. Spoon the flapjack mixture into the lined tin and press down using the back of a spoon.

For a two-oven Aga; hang the tin on the bottom set of runners of the roasting oven and put the cold shelf on the second set of runners from the bottom of the oven. Bake for 20-25 minutes. For a three- or four-oven Aga; hang the tin on the second set of runners from the bottom of the baking oven and bake the flapjacks for 30-35 minutes.

To insure the flapjacks are evenly baked it may be a good idea to turn the tin round after 20 minutes, this depends upon your Aga. When cooked, the flapjacks will be a pale golden brown. Cut the flapjacks into squares whilst still warm and in the tin. Allow to cool and firm.

Mincemeat Flapjacks

Mincemeat is such a versatile ingredient at this
time of year. It's perfect for topping and filling
so many wonderful sweet things, not least these
very simple but very tasty flapjacks.

Mincemeat flapjacks, page 171

Kitchenalia
(Items To Make Life Easier)

These are the bits and pieces of equipment that I find most useful at Christmas (and other times of the year). A lot of items may seem expensive, but if you look after them they will last for years. I put most of my equipment in the dishwasher, but never the Aga baking trays, hard, anodised saucepans, or any cast-iron.

An Aga kettle.

Aga large or small roasting tin, depending on the size of your bird or joint of meat.

Aga large and small hard anodised baking tray to fit on the runners.

Bake-O-Glide starter pack or pieces cut to fit the above tins.

Milk saucepan, ideally an Aga non-stick saucepan.

Selection of Aga saucepans to use on the top and in the ovens. Sizes to suit your family.

A good quality cake tin. If you only buy one, choose an Aga spring-release tin for versatility.

Aga cast-iron ridged pan, perfect for steak, fish, vegetables and fruit.

Aga cast-iron Danish pot, perfect for mulled wine and soups.

Mini muffin tins, at least two, for mince pies and canapés.

Timer. Which Aga-owner could be without one?

Carving knife and fork, the best you can afford, with a steel – this will make carving easier.

Microplane medium-grater. These modern graters make grating orange rind and cheese so much easier.

Giant meat-lifting forks. These will ensure the turkey doesn't end up on the floor!

A balloon whisk and flour shaker, perfect for gravy.

Finally, if you love cooking – who doesn't when you own an Aga! – a Kitchen Aid mixer and blender are real labour-saving devices. They are available in a range of colours which look stunning.

Appendix 1

Whole Turkey and Turkey Crown
(whole bird with legs removed)

Fast Method
(2, 3 and 4 oven Aga cookers)
Rub liberally with butter. Place in the Aga roasting tin, on a grill rack if liked. Hang from the lowest set of runners in the roasting oven for one hour until nicely browned. The top table opposite shows the total fast method roasting times.

Medium Method
(3 and 4 oven Aga cookers only)
Rub liberally with butter. Place in the Aga roasting tin, on a grill rack if liked. Hang from the lowest set of runners in the roasting oven for up to one hour until nicely browned. After the first hour in the Roasting Oven, transfer the turkey to the Baking Oven to finish cooking, for the *additional* times in the *middle* table opposite.

Slow Method
(2, 3 and 4 oven Aga cookers)
Rub liberally with butter. Place in the Aga roasting tin without a grill rack. Roast on the floor of the roasting oven for up to one hour. After the first hour in the roasting oven, transfer the turkey to the simmering oven to finish cooking, for the *additional* times in the *bottom* table opposite.

FAST METHOD (2, 3 AND 4 OVEN AGA COOKERS)

8-12lb	3.6-5.4kg	$1^3/_4$-2 hours
12-16lb	5.4-7.25kg	2-$2^1/_2$ hours
16-20lb	7.25-9.0kg	$2^1/_2$-3 hours
20-24lb	9.0-10.8kg	3-$3^1/_2$ hours
24-28lb	10.8-12.6kg	$3^1/_2$-4 hours

MEDIUM METHOD (3 AND 4 OVEN AGA COOKERS ONLY)

8-12lb	3.6-5.4kg	$1^1/_2$-$2^1/_2$ hours
12-16lb	5.4-7.25kg	$2^1/_2$-$3^1/_2$ hours
16-20lb	7.25-9.0kg	$3^1/_2$-$4^1/_2$ hours
20-24lb	9.0-10.8kg	$4^1/_2$-$5^1/_2$ hours
24-28lb	10.8-12.6kg	$5^1/_2$-$6^1/_2$ hours

SLOW METHOD (2, 3 AND 4 OVEN AGA COOKERS)

8-12lb	3.6-5.4kg	3-5 hours
12-16lb	5.4-7.25kg	5-$7^1/_2$ hours
16-20lb	7.25-9.0kg	$7^1/_2$-10 hours
20-24lb	9.0-10.8kg	10-$12^1/_2$ hours
24-28lb	10.8-12.6kg	$12^1/_2$-15 hours

Appendix 2

Gammon Cooking Times

1-1½kg / 2-3¼lb	2½ hours
1¾ -2¼kg / 4-5lb	3 hours
2½-3¼kg / 5½-7lb	3½ hours
3½-4kg / 8-9lb	4½ hours
4½-5kg / 10-11lb	5½ hours
5½-6kg / 12-13lb	6½ hours
6½-6¾kg / 14-15lb	7½ hours
7¼kg and over / 16lb	overnight or 12 hours

Index

almond and broccoli stir-fry 110
apples:
    glazed parsnip purée 64
    guinea fowl with prunes 77
    sauce 36
    stuffing with potato 34
apricot mincemeat 23
aubergine: tian 113

bacon: devils on horseback 145
beef:
    mini Yorkshire puddings 136
    pie with venison and cranberry 76
    roast 56
beetroot:
    risotto with red wine 101
    roasted with goats' cheese 105
biscuits:
    brandy snaps 130
    olive oil crackers 149
    petits fours 157
    shortbread 27
braised red cabbage with raspberry vinegar 68
brandy butter 41
brandy snaps 130
bread:
    bruschettas 143
    sauce 35
Brie: with stuffed peppers 98
broccoli: stir-fry with almonds 110
bruschettas 143
Brussels sprouts with chestnuts 52
bubble and squeak cakes 169
Buche de Noel 123
butter: brandy 42
butter-roasted cabbage 83
butterbeans: mash with sugar-glazed gammon
    92

cabbage:
    butter-roasted 83
    cheesy bubble and squeak cakes 169
    see also red cabbage
cakes:
    Buche de Noel 123
    chocolate 19
    Christmas 17
    Christmas fruit and nut 18
    gateau Pithiviers 122
    gorgeous chocolate 121
    mini cranberry and walnut muffins 133
    rich sticky gingerbread 129
    Stollen 118
    see also marzipan; royal icing
canapés:
    bruschettas 143
    chilli salt squid 152
    devils on horseback 145
    mini roast beef Yorkshire puddings 136
    parsnip spikes 138
    pastry squares with ricotta and tomato 142
    pesto palmiers 153
    sesame seed tarts with smoked salmon
        mousse 139
    spiced potato wedges 137
    Thai fishcakes with cucumber relish 151
caramel oranges 132
casseroles: venison with pickled walnuts 74
celeriac: soup with garlic 108
cheese:
    hot feta cheese 104
    jalousie with ham 170
    leek and Stilton soup 106
    mascarpone and gorgonzola tart with
        balsamic onions 103
    Parmesan and mustard parsnips 85
    pastry squares with ricotta and tomato 142
    stuffed peppers with Brie 98
    see also goats' cheese

Traditional Aga Christmas

cheesy bubble and squeak cakes 169
chestnuts:
    Brussels sprouts 52
    stuffing 33
chicken:
    citrus with red onions 90
    stir-fry with mango 89
    tatin 164
chicken liver and cranberry terrine with
    cranberry confit 88
chilli salt squid 152
chocolate:
    Buche de Noel 123
    cake 19, 121
    tea pots 154
Christmas cake 17
Christmas countdown 46
Christmas fruit and nut cake 18
Christmas fruit ice cream 28
Christmas nut loaf 62
Christmas pudding:
    Granny's 12
    light 14
citrus chicken with red onions 90
confits: cranberry with chicken liver terrine 88
corn and ginger soup 109
courgettes: marinated 112
cranberries:
    mincemeat 25
    muffins with walnut 133
    pie with venison and beef 76
    plait with marzipan 156
    sauce 36
    terrine with chicken liver and cranberry
        confit 88
cream of celeriac and garlic soup 108
creamed turkey and ham soup 162
cucumber: relish with Thai fishcakes 151
custards: marsala 28

desserts *see* puddings
devils on horseback 145
dips 148
dried fruit:
Christmas fruit and nut cake 18
Christmas fruit ice cream 28
stuffing 33
see also mincemeat; prunes

equipment 176

fennel gratin 114
fish:
    chilli salt squid 152
    smoked mackerel dip 148
    Thai fishcakes with cucumber relish 151
    see also salmon; smoked salmon
flapjacks: mincemeat 171
forcemeat stuffing 32
fruit
    apricot mincemeat 23
    chicken and mango stir-fry 89
    stuffing 33
    see also apples; cranberries; dried fruit;
        oranges

gammon:
    cooking times 180
    glazed 39
    sugar-glazed with butterbean mash 92
    see also ham
gateau Pithiviers 122
giblet stock 37
glazed prune tart 120
goats' cheese:
    with roast beetroot 105
    roulade with smoked salmon 97
goose: roast 61
gorgeous chocolate cake 121
Granny's Christmas pudding 12

gratins:
  fennel 114
  potato and horseradish
gravy 50
guinea fowl with prunes and apples 77

ham:
  creamed turkey soup 162
  jalousie with cheese 170
herb-stuffed leg of lamb 73
horseradish:
  gratin with potato 79
  sauce 35
hot feta cheese 104

ice cream: Christmas fruit 28
icing, royal 15

lamb, herb-stuffed 73
leek and Stilton soup 106
Light Christmas pudding 14
lime-glazed winter vegetables 67

mango: stir-fry with chicken 89
marinated courgettes 112
marsala custard 28
marzipan 15
  plait with cranberry 156
mascarpone and gorgonzola tart with balsamic
  onions 103
mashed potatoes Bolognese style 78
meat:
  devils on horseback 145
  herb-stuffed leg of lamb 73
  pork fillets with puy lentils 93
  see also beef; gammon; ham; venison
meringue:
  Pavlova 126
  roulade 28
mince pies 20

mincemeat:
  apricot 23
  cranberry 25
  flapjacks 171
  sugar-free 24
mini cranberry and walnut muffins 133

nuts:
  almond and broccoli stir-fry 110
  Christmas fruit and nut cake 18
  Christmas nut loaf 62
  spiced 144
  see also walnuts

olive oil crackers 149
onions: balsamic with mascarpone and
  gorgonzola tart 103; see also red onions
oranges:
  caramel 132
  pheasant breast with walnut 72

parsnips:
  with Parmesan and mustard 85
  purée 64
  roast winter roots 65
  spikes 138
pasta: tagliatelli in a lemony sauce 96
pastry:
  cranberry and marzipan plait 156
  ham and cheese jalousie 170
  mascarpone and gorgonzola tart 103
  pesto palmiers 153
  salmon en croute 95
  squares with ricotta and tomato 142
  turkey 163
  see also tarts
Pavlova 126
pesto palmiers 153
petits fours 157
pheasant:

breasts with orange and walnut 72
roast 55
pies:
    turkey or chicken tatin 164
    venison, beef and cranberry 76
pork fillet with puy lentils 93
potatoes:
    cheesy bubble and squeak cakes 169
    gratin with horseradish 79
    mashed Bolognese style 78
    roast 50
    spiced wedges 137
    stuffing with apple 34
poultry:
    guinea fowl with prunes and apples 77
    roast goose 61
    see also chicken; pheasant; turkey
prunes:
devils on horseback 145
glazed tart 120
guinea fowl with apples 77
puddings:
    chocolate tea pots 154
    glazed prune tart 120
    Granny's Christmas pudding 12
    light Christmas pudding 14
    meringue roulade 28
    Pavlova 126
    trifle 40
puy lentils: pork fillet 93

red cabbage:
    braised with raspberry vinegar 68
    spicy 82
red onions: citrus chicken 90
red peppers: stuffed with Brie 98
relish: cucumber with Thai fishcakes 151
rice:
    beetroot and red wine risotto 101
    wild mushroom risotto 100

rich sticky gingerbread 129
roast winter roots 65
roasting methods 47, 49, 178, 179
roulades:
    Buche de Noel 123
    smoked salmon and goats' cheese 97
royal icing 15

sage and onion stuffing 32
salmon
    en croute 95
    fishcakes with lemon butter sauce 166
    soufflé 167
    see also smoked salmon
sauces:
    apple 36
    bread 35
    cranberry 36
    gravy 50
    horseradish 35
    lemon butter 166
    sherry 43
sesame seed tarts with smoked salmon mousse
    139
sherry sauce 41
shortbread 27
smoked mackerel dip 148
smoked salmon:
    dip 148
    mousse with sesame seed tarts 139
    roulade with goats' cheese 97
soufflés: salmon 167
soups:
    corn and ginger 109
    cream of celeriac and garlic 108
    creamed turkey and ham 162
    leek and Stilton 106
spiced nuts 144
spiced potato wedges 137
spicy red cabbage 82

squid: chilli salt 152
stir-fries:
  almond and broccoli 110
  chicken and mango 89
stock: giblet 37
Stollen 118
stuffed peppers with Brie 98
stuffing:
  chestnut 33
  forcemeat 32
  fruit 33
  potato and apple 34
  sage and onion 32
sugar-free mincemeat 24
sugar-glazed gammon with butterbean mash
  92

tagliatelli in a lemony sauce 96
tarts:
  mascarpone and gorgonzola with balsamic
    onions 103
  prune 120
  sesame seed with smoked salmon mousse
    139
terrines: chicken liver and cranberry 88
Thai fishcakes with cucumber relish 151
tian of aubergines 113
trifle 40
turkey:
  creamed soup with ham 162
  pastries 163
  preparation 47
  roasting, fast 47, 178, 179
  roasting, medium 47, 49, 178, 179
  roasting, slow 49, 178, 179
  tatin 164

vegetables:
  almond and broccoli stir-fry 110
  aubergine tian 113
  balsamic onions with mascarpone and
    gorgonzola tart 103
  Brussels sprouts with chestnuts 52
  butterbean mash with gammon 92
  citrus chicken with red onions 90
  corn and ginger soup 109
  cream of celeriac and garlic soup 108
  fennel gratin 114
  leek and Stilton soup 106
  lime-glazed winter vegetables 67
  marinated courgettes 112
  roast winter roots 65
  stuffed peppers with Brie 98
  wild mushroom risotto 100
  see also beetroot; cabbage; parsnips;
    potatoes; red cabbage
venison:
casserole with pickled walnuts 74
pie with beef and cranberry 76
roast 59

walnuts:
  muffins with cranberry 133
  pheasant breast with orange 72
  pickled with venison casserole
wild mushroom risotto 100

Yorkshire puddings 58
  mini roast beef 136

Acknowledgements

Christmas comes but once a year, though to Aga demonstrators it seems more often. Bookings for the following year's Christmas demonstrations in the shops are taken as soon as a Christmas season is over. There is also a long lead-up time, so making Christmas pudding and mincemeat starts, for me, in September. All this is because Christmas is such an important time for Aga owners: something upon which I have often pondered. Perhaps it's because many people have their Aga installed during the run up to Christmas and are worried about fitting everything in and running out of heat during that final big cook, although such worries tend to be short-lived. I think most experienced Aga owners feel the Aga to be at the heart of the family and know that it won't let them down. So this book is for all the lovely Aga owners I have met over the years doing all those Christmas demonstrations, and for those I can help and reassure in the future.

I visit many Aga shops, but for several years now, it has felt as though I have moved into the Cardiff Aga shop at Christmas. Lorraine, Debbie, Caroline and Linda give a wonderful service to their customers and we all enjoy the Christmas demonstrations. Thank you Cardiff, in particular, for asking for this book.

Thank you to Jon, Matt and Meg at Absolute Press who have come up with the idea and encouraged me through the difficult times and for their inspired book design and layout.

Thank you to my family for testing all the recipes. Hugo and friends who have eaten turkey for Sunday lunch when they would have preferred something else; Dominic, who has eaten Christmas cake on the hottest day in June and Hanna, who has put up with all the dried fruits she really doesn't like. My husband Geoff and all our friends have once again been invited to try all sorts of strange mixtures as part of the continual testing process. Geoff, thank you for helping with all the washing-up that won't fit in the dishwasher.

I would like to dedicate this book to my cousin Brian Timms who died during its preparation. He always loved Christmas and the opportunity it provided for spending time with family and friends.